9t

Robert A Swratill

12/13/09

This Page Intentionally Left Blank –
Just Like the Paychecks of the Workers

This Page Intentionally Left Blank – Just Like the Paychecks of the Workers

By Robert S. Swiatek

Aventine Press

Published by Aventine Press
1023 4th Ave #204
San Diego CA, 92101
www.aventinepress.com

ISBN: 1-59330-500-1

Printed in the United States of America

This book is dedicated to those who have to choose between being homeless or being hungry while defrocked CEOs are stuck with a severance pay of a mere seven figures.

Introduction

Not long ago, *24/7* actually became a word. Don't blame me; it certainly wasn't my idea. I think it's time to say Sayonara to it, since it just hasn't worked and probably should more realistically be described as *el toro crappo*. How about replacing it with *30/15*? The *30* represents the number of hours in the new workweek and the *15* stands for the number of dollars in the new minimum wage.

The sixty-hour week at the factory has only led to stress, heart attacks, stomach illnesses and other health problems as well as not really getting the job done. It really doesn't matter what kind of work you do, no one can be productive putting in that many hours a week. People who lived a century ago would remark that sixty is nothing as they were forced to endure eighty-hour stints. That boils down to sixteen hours a day for a five-day week or in excess of eleven hours for working every day of the week ending in a "y." I cannot imagine how they put up with those ludicrous hours. That is one of the reasons why our grandparents and great grandparents had such short life spans.

In *Soul of a Citizen: Living with Conviction in a Cynical Time*, Paul Rogat Loeb, states, "We should be able to earn a living wage without sacrificing our psychological, spiritual and sometimes even physical well-being by giving over our entire lives to our jobs." Ro Donahue – my supervisor on the last contract I had – was right on the money when she said that family and home life came first and then work followed in importance.

Realistically, how much work do you think employers get out of those who are on the job for a "mere" forty hours a week? Even that number of hours is problematical and causes burnout. Since no one is physically capable of being truly productive for so many hours in a week – I'll get to why later – why does management still insist on the practice? With technology, shouldn't the length of the workweek have decreased over the years, rather than skyrocketed to such heights? I witnessed the shortening of those hours in my experiences on the farm, in the factory and in the office and this decrease seemed typical for a while. Unfortunately, once the minimum of thirty-five hours was attained, it didn't stay there for long but instead started climbing back up and got to where it is today, which is over forty hours a week, even though the contract said forty.

The good news is that the Senate passed a bill for a thirty-hour workweek and the House was all set to do the same. The bad news is that Roosevelt felt it wasn't a good idea. That failure was in 1933, so it's time to pass this legislation, even if it takes three quarters of a century to do it. At the same time raise the hourly pay to fifteen dollars an hour, since the current one is minimal in every sense of the word, and it shouldn't come in increments of a dime each year for a hundred years. There has not been a boost in the minimum wage in nine years – it hasn't been raised since 1997. In that same period, the Congress has approved its own pay increases eight times. For their efforts over that period, I feel most of them should surrender at least part of their salaries.

Being the richest nation on earth, there should be no problem finding the dough to make *30/15* a reality. There's plenty of cash available if companies can accept corporate welfare and give incompetent CEOs millions of dollars and say, "good-bye and don't come back." These departing, deficient dictators should be handed a pen as a souvenir and should be sued for back pay. Amazingly, the *30/15* concept can actually increase company profits, which those in management with butter beans for brains obviously haven't figured out. Arguments by posturing politicians or money minded moguls of the business world against this progressive thought are nothing more than spin, which should be relegated to *Wheel of Fortune.*

Obviously, much elaboration is needed and *This Page Intentionally Left Blank – Just Like the Paychecks of the*

Workers will try to do that. It is a book about work, which evolved into social justice concerns of *30/15*. In 2003, I had my third book published, *Tick Tock, Don't Stop: A Manual for Workaholics*, which got some good reviews. I wrote it because I saw too many people struggling to stay ahead in the rat race. Some labored from dawn to dusk, even though they retired some time ago. Others stayed on the job while they could have easily afforded to retire. Unfortunately, the book described hasn't sold enough copies because things in the business world have only deteriorated and people are still struggling, no matter how they try to make a living. The long workweek and the small paychecks have a great deal to do with that.

Today the gap in compensation between upper management and those who actually produce the goods – whether it is a product or a service – is higher than it has ever been. On the average, according to what I read, those at the top receive 411 times the salary of those in the work force – that multiplier is probably too low. The employees' plight is so desperate that I am convinced that slavery was never abolished, as downsizing and outsourcing seem to confirm.

Laborers in the Third World, who endure endless hours today in the sweat shops creating goods that sell for hundreds of dollars in the United States while they are paid under a dollar an hour, are no better off than those who suffered in the heat on the plantations for too many years before the Civil War restored some of their dignity. You can be unemployed, underemployed or over employed and underpaid – working two or more jobs to pay for food and shelter. You could have a job but no home. Having to decide between being homeless or without food is not a choice anyone in America or anywhere else should have to make.

People in corporate America are better off than workers who have to figure a way to make ends meet on anywhere from $5 to $9 an hour, but their lives are no picnics either. Many don't have the luxury of joining a labor union when they really need one because those organizations are becoming as rare as slide rules and balanced budgets. Management won't allow workers to even talk to the unions without being booted out the door.

Given the vast wealth of our nation, there is no reason for there to be poverty, homelessness, unemployed people, underemployed people or people working sixty hours a week and still not making ends meet. I have to ask these questions of the filthy rich, "How much money can you spend?" and "Have you no sense of decency or compassion?" Marian Wright Edelman remarks, "We are going to have to develop a concept of enough at the top and at the bottom, so that the necessities of the many are not sacrificed for the luxuries of the few."

Our society cannot exist and prosper under the conditions that we see today. This effort will get more into social justice issues, for which the corporations and politicians seem not to care. I hope this book gives you a few more laughs than *Tick Tock, Don't Stop* provided. I also hope that more people will get a chance to read it, although it's not too late to pick up a copy of the book that was published in 2003. By buying either book, you may not be able to retire, but you should be able to do so sooner and you won't become a millionaire, but you should have a richer life.

This Page Intentionally Left Blank is written to entice readers into action about the main thrust of the book. A replacement of *24/7* with *30/15* will go a long way to making our lives better. I add other thoughts that are tied in to the workweek and minimum wage, such as how to retire sooner. I talked to a friend of mine who said she was having a hard time adjusting to being retired. I told her that she probably loved her work too much and if she had hated it, she wouldn't have had such a difficult time away from it. I hope she gets over this feeling, as this should be a better time for her. I talk to a lot of people after they retire that feel so good about the change that they wish they had left the work force sooner.

There are other issues I discuss related to *30/15* such as slavery, an alternative to hard work without laziness, married priests, where the money went, moving garage sales, why we despise work and why the hours in the week have gotten longer rather than shorter, especially with all those technological advances. This book also has thoughts on immigration, the idea of thresholds, artists as well as education and its impacts on work and some changes that we need in institutions of learning.

The book argues for a return of Sunday as a day of rest – I'm all for that and do my best to keep my PC (Pain in the Crotch) turned off on that day. I point out conclusive cases of where work can kill you and tell of speed bumps and potholes in the road, some of which you may not have been aware. I talk about materialism, health care, unnecessary work, which I especially despise, and offer some of my adventures and a few other topics to entertain as well as enlighten you.

The book wouldn't be complete without some suggestions to help us change the climate in corporape (many workers feel violated) America to make our lives better, including an excel spreadsheet so you can see how much cash is flowing out your wallet. There are recommendations for government, unions, the press and corporations but I also add a few ideas for people as individuals. As bad as things are, there is the hope that changes can be made to improve the profits of the companies as well as the lives of the working class so that we can retire sooner and also have a few years to enjoy that time.

As far as the main title goes, those first five words are familiar to all of us. I first encountered them at Nestle Foods, when I was perusing computer manuals – I was having difficulty sleeping. We can probably thank IBM for the start of my book title, but if you've run into these words somewhere, you'll realize that you can't hand over the sheet of paper with those five words to someone who wants to borrow something to write on. It really isn't blank, but apparently two things are: the brain of the person who came up with the idea as well as the supervisor who sanctioned these five words. If there is nothing on a page, I think people can figure that out and it doesn't need explaining. Did the corporation actually pay these "innovators?" I hope not.

This Page Intentionally Left Blank has nothing to do with scandals in the Nation's Capital during 2006, although the book, of necessity, isn't apolitical. Those first five words of the title refer to the paychecks of the workers as well as the feelings of the average Joe and Joan on Saturday because the workweek is too long and the wages too minimal. It refers to the emptiness of the factories and businesses that have had jobs shipped to India and China. It represents the look of those in hospitals who have worked too many hours for too little pay. These words stand for the unnecessary work that people do while meaningful endeavors are put aside, never to be initiated.

The subtitle I originally thought about was, *30/15 not 24/7*, which would have been fine, since that is certainly a theme here. This work is a plea for a drastic change to eradicate *24/7* from the dictionary as well as from our lives, once and for all time. The *30/15* is a much better idea that workers in the United States can live with.

I need to give a few other words of warning: some of the words you see in this book you may not find in any dictionary. One of the advantages of being a writer is the privilege of using clichés, alliteration and also the option of ending sentences in prepositions. This you could never get away with in English class. I can also use combinations of letters that actually aren't real words. This is done for a few laughs, which are definitely needed at a time when there is so much despair in the working environment. Despite that, all is not hopeless as we have the ability to come with up solutions for just about any problem.

Table of contents

1
The 60s and other reasons for hating work

Each of us has a list of things that we absolutely hate. I hope this doesn't get into more than four or five for you because if so, you may need to get some help; you're a pessimist and your life is bound for trouble. If you are really concerned, remember that I used the word "absolutely." I have four on my list, three of which are appropriate to the idea of work and the first two will be covered in this chapter. The first is the 1960s, with all the turbulence and turmoil. It was a time of unrest when we witnessed the Vietnam War as well as the assassination of John F. Kennedy, Malcolm X, Martin Luther King, Jr., Robert Kennedy and Medgar Evers as well as a few other political leaders who may not have been favorable to certain governments. *Remembering America: a Voice from the Sixties* by Richard N. Goodwin is almost 550 pages long, but it's a book about that bothersome decade that should be read by everyone, even if you aren't older than dirt and weren't around or simply were asleep at that time.

I hated the 60s for other reasons as well. Besides the issues mentioned above, it was a time when I began my college career and the majority of the decade was a time when I was in school. For some, college can be a fun time with all the partying and beer flowing but I was one person who didn't believe in studying for tests and giving back everything that my teachers wanted to hear. Parrots are fine for pets, but they have no place in the classroom, unless they know the answers to the professor's questions. I wanted the education I was paying for, not all that time that I had to spend doing unnecessary papers and projects, studying for tests and recovering from hangovers, but I will get more into that later – not the day after part.

In addition, I was working to help pay for my education. Fortunately, my parents provided me with food and shelter all this time and didn't ask for a penny for these things during my years in college. I should also add that what I paid for one semester's tuition then would not have been sufficient to buy the textbooks for my niece Elizabeth, who graduated in 2006 from the University at Buffalo, where I spent some time in the 1960s. The job that I had for eight long years all through undergraduate school, grad school and even when I got my first "real" job as a teacher was at one supermarket in Cheektowaga, a suburb of Buffalo. I should mention that the second thing that I hate is the supermarket, and that may be because of my extended stay there, even though it was only "part-time." Anyone who works and goes to school realizes that it has to get better than that! Unfortunately, there are very few people who aren't trapped in that regimen.

Had I been a genius who could have gotten A's without studying or going to class, things may have been different. Needless to say, I had to work at getting passing grades, both in college and graduate school. One factor may have been staying at home as it may have been different had I lived on campus. Of course, that option costs money so it really wasn't much of a choice for me. The really hard part of this combination school and work existence is that there is no time to rest as school usually involves five days a week – Monday through Friday – and Saturday for me was eight hours doing the grocery thing. This left only Sunday, which was the day to catch up on schoolwork. There's no rest for the wicked!

As bad as things might appear under these circumstances, it gets worse if you have to work on Sunday doing inventory at the store. That may only involve four or five hours but there were a few days in my freshman year in college when the supermarket was actually open on Sunday and I was scheduled to work eight hours. This leaves you no free time at all, even if you plan to ignore class reading assignments, studying and doing papers.

When I recall my undergraduate days, there was one time I really looked forward to: the mid-semester break. It was only one week long and I doubt that this anticipation was on my mind during my first two years in college. That's because I was young and foolish and the "burnout" factor had yet to reach me. Junior and senior year were different, though. That one-week period meant that I had no worries about opening a book for class, studying for exams, doing homework or any projects. My only concern was the few hours that I spent in the grocery store. You might say my mind went on vacation.

My pet peeves are intertwined as is education and the work of our lives. We go to school to be able to get a "good job," which on graduation may be difficult to land. Nevertheless, to be able to go to school, someone has to pay for it and that falls on the family. Most of us are not blessed with the resources to be able to attend classes without getting part-time employment. We just can't glide through the process by going to parties in the dormitories – now replaced by the condominiums of student housing. That is not a financial possibility for the majority of students, even with a full scholarship. Just buying books will require going to the bank for a mortgage! That's an exaggeration but paying for an education will require many months of loan payments once graduation day passes. In *Downsized But Not Out* in *The Nation* magazine of November 6, 2006, Barbara Ehrenreich and Tamara Draut state that those who borrow to pay for college are $20,000 in the red after they graduate. Keep in mind that this number is an average, so that what some owe will be much greater than that.

My hate relationship had to do with the number of hours that seemed to overwhelm me. Assuming I had twenty hours of class each week – that could be a bit low – and I worked the same number of hours at the meat market, you can see that the sum happens to be forty hours, which you might say isn't bad at all. However, you have forgotten the fact that I may have been required to do some chores at home. Living with your parents isn't always free! Suppose that involved two hours each week. The other consideration is schoolwork, which could easily be eight hours – I think that's way too low for college – but as you can observe, I am now stuck with at least fifty hours for each seven-day period. I will spend an entire chapter later on the much too long workweek today and what can be done about it.

There are other reasons within our society why we hate work. One has to do with people looking over our shoulders – you probably know that I am referring to management. In my case I got hit from both sides as I had managers at work but also teachers who filled the same role. I had a myriad of bosses at the store and by the time I left after eight years, I noticed that many of them stayed out of my hair, but initially there were a few that made life difficult. One superior in particular was a bit deficient in people skills – something really necessary in that position. Perhaps, this was his first assignment as a manager. At the same time he wasn't that great at ordering stock, which I expected was a minimum requirement for that job as a head honcho.

As far as teachers go, your life in college can be much more enjoyable if you have instructors who care about you and do everything in their power to make sure you succeed. These are the people who will bring you up to levels of achievement that you never felt you could reach. If you are stuck with lousy professors who care only about their salary, you will have a challenging time and you won't look forward to class. Since there is a huge correlation between education and work, I will get into more detail in a later chapter.

Once you get into the work place after graduation, your boss returns as a factor. If he or she stands over your shoulder for every little thing, you may want to try to find either a new department or a new job. If he hired you because of your potential but doesn't trust you to do the job yourself without direction, he doesn't belong in management. The sad part might be that you saw great potential at this company.

Another reason for hating your job has to do with mismatches. Say you got a degree in mathematics and now you sign a contract to teach high school English; you may have a tough time. A person I know studied psychology and wound up teaching elementary school. I don't think this individual was that happy there and would have been better off getting a degree in elementary education – at least prior to getting this assignment, or else a job in psychology or some related field.

Other reasons for despising work have to do with jobs that are boring, meaningless or created. As a consultant, I was usually stuck with the tasks that the full-time people didn't want – the maintenance endeavors. One of the biggest projects of this kind was Y2K, which I saw as a great challenge. In my eyes, it should never have happened in the first place. On one occasion I worked for a company and developed the order entry system specifications and later returned as a consultant to actually do the programming. That was my favorite contract. Unfortunately, those situations are rare for a self-employed person.

For boring jobs and managers that are hard to take, a nice paycheck can ease the pain. The excitement comes in when one realizes that retirement may be around the corner, provided dollars are invested along the way, rather than as an indulgence in unlimited buying. Of course, there are many instances where money doesn't mean much. Recently I was at a party and one of my classmates mentioned that he was offered a few thousand dollars to re-enlist. He decided that he had his fill of the service and no amount of cash would entice him to remain there.

Dissatisfaction with the job could have to do with the amount of compensation one receives. That will always be a factor, but as I mentioned, in many cases people understand that money doesn't buy happiness and no amount of pay will get an individual to work at some particular job, based on various factors.

Another reason why we hate work has to do with "control." I'm sure you've seen the "soup-nazi" episode on Seinfeld and realize what kind of hate was created in that restaurant. The same applies to work and something else enters into the equation: trust. If there is respect between the worker and his superior, control is present, but it is minimal and the worker will be pleased with his employment situation. After all, each of us – whether we admit it or not – wants to be controlled in some way. However, things get out of hand when there is too much control.

On many occasions I have heard full time staff denigrate the consultants, insisting they got paid more than they were worth. This is definitely true in some cases, but certainly not all. In reply, the contractor might have asked that person why she didn't become a consultant, if it was so financially rewarding. The reason the accuser stayed where she was had to do with control, since her full-time job represented the amount that she was comfortable with. A consultant needs a great deal of discipline when his paycheck arrives. He must keep in mind that the current contract may end at any time. The salaried individual doesn't want this worry, no matter what that alternate opportunity pays. There are other concerns, which I will get into shortly.

Apprehension affects us at home when we have a task that has to get done, even if we don't get paid for it. In many cases we put it off simply because we can't quite get motivated to do it. It may have been on our work list for weeks, but apprehension for some reason keeps us from beginning the job. We just may not have a comfort level, so we can't begin. Once we get started, it may not be long before we are done and we might wonder why we hesitated in the first place. This same feeling hits us at the office when we have four assignments and we prioritize them – if our boss allows us that option. We do the job that appears easiest first. That will never change with the passage of time.

Politics and favoritism enter into why we aren't too happy with some assignments. If you spend time with the company and do the best you can and someone else gets the promotion that you wanted even though she showed neither the drive nor effort to match yours, you won't be too thrilled. It's called politics, not one of my favorite parts of work. Luckily, being a consultant shields you from some of this aspect, but you can't avoid it completely. There have been times when I felt like I was back in grade school based on some of management's practices – maybe *practices* is a good word in this case since they're still feeling their way. That approach won't keep many employees around very long.

Getting into the work force can be done by being your own boss or working for someone else, but either will be a gross undertaking. In each, you will have to commute to work, not the greatest time before and after the workday, not with the congestion on the highways. There are other challenges as well, many of which I touched on previously in my first book on work.

Being self-employed means you have no boss except yourself, but what if you can't stand him? You're really up the creek without a paddle, which sounds like a good title for a book – I may want to add another word to it. The difficulty of working on your own is finding work as well as the adequate remuneration for your effort. That is where the consulting firm comes in, but now you have to share the billing with those sponges. On those many occasions, I felt I had two bosses. One was the manager at the corporation and the other was the dude from the consulting firm who got me the contract. In most cases, the latter didn't even stop in to see me at the office – which I didn't mind, as long as I got those checks. On other occasions, they showed up more than I felt was necessary – especially if they didn't buy me lunch.

As a consultant I was rather lucky as there were a few occasions when my contract ended and the next Monday I started another. That may have been an instance when I would have welcomed a break but it just wasn't an option. On the other hand, there were a few occasions when I had long breaks that

I really didn't want. I also had to get my own health insurance and there weren't any paid holidays, sick time, personal days or vacation. If you didn't go in to the office, you didn't get paid for the day. The only time when you are allowed to not show up is in the event of death. You still needed to give two weeks notice. Such is the life of a consultant.

The consulting profession has a few unwritten rules, one of which is that contractors never take sick days. This is based on the way billing occurs, as I mentioned earlier. So even if she is suffering from some kind of flu or virus, her duty is to be at the office, no matter what. This appearance can be beneficial as full-time staff may wind up with exactly what the consultant had and have to stay home. The full-time staff can take a sick day, since they get paid for it. An extra added bonus is that this action could result in a longer stay at the corporation for the self-employed individual, since there will be a bit more work to get done with all the germs spread around by the consultant. By the same token, consultants should remind the full-time people of how bad work is and encourage them to take days off here and there, thus enabling the consultant to extend his contract even further.

You could also be self-employed and open a restaurant but I wouldn't recommend that since your problems might be never-ending. That doesn't even touch on the possibility of failure for lack of customers despite a great location, good menu and fantastic reviews. I love to cook – you can read about that in my first book, *The Read My Lips Cookbook: a Culinary Journey of Memorable Meals* – but I have no desire to open up an eating establishment. The hours are much too long, even if you are your own boss.

Going it on your own is tough. You have to find the clients who will buy your product or enlist your services. That has nothing to do with your degrees or skills, but in getting the message out. In not having to put up with the stress of getting on the highway or being in the office, you may have inadvertently created stress with a shortage of customers and no consequent cash flow. You have to have the latter for food and shelter. Today's employees – whether self-employed or not – don't have it easy by any stretch of the imagination.

2
A reasonable workweek

On April 6, 1933, a bill was passed by the Senate to establish a thirty-hour workweek and the House of representatives was on the verge of passing it. Unfortunately for all of us, it didn't quite make it, as the Roosevelt administration – you figure out which one – didn't approve of the idea. You can read more about this failure in *Take Back Your Time*, a book of essays on work edited by John de Graaf. Throughout history, the numbers of hours that made up the weekly grind has generally decreased. This is true for the majority of the working class even though some did put in more hours than the norm. Somewhere along the way in the last quarter century or so, this number started to rise once more to the point that sixty hours seemed to be a "reasonable" request of employees.

I worked on a truck farm in the late 1950s, including Saturdays during school in the spring and fall. During the summer, we worked eight hours each day from Monday through Friday as well as a half-day on Saturday, when we got paid – in cash. Farmer George probably figured I didn't have a checking account or else he was printing his own money. The cash payment also gave me the opportunity to skim a few pennies off the top if I had to turn over my pay to my parents. At that time and for a few years to follow, most of the jobs involved a workweek of forty hours. When I began teaching, my day of instruction may have been from 8 am to 2 pm, but it generally involved more than eight hours, depending on circumstances. After all, it is a good idea to prepare a lesson before class – your department chairman might observe you and you don't want him to get the wrong idea – and I did volunteer at times for after-school activities. I never did do any time calculations as to what I really earned by the hour, as I was too busy preparing for geometry class.

In the summer of 1975, I began a new career in the business world of computers and I was required to work a thirty-seven and one half hour week. Assuming this constant progression for the better, you can see that today, if the maximum labor time happened to be thirty hours per week, that number would be appropriate and fitting and not unexpected. However, we know that this idea is like seeing an honest politician. It just isn't happening since employers are demanding sixty hours per week from the help.

I will get into some of the reasons why today we are burdened by this long week – if we have a job. For now, let me try to show why the sixty-hour workweek just isn't good for anyone – the reply Gary Schandling gave after being questioned by his lady friend after an evening of engaging with her without buying her a ring, if you know what I mean. This long week might have come about because a project at the office had three employees working forty hours each. A decree came down from upper management to cut staff in the group, going from three to two workers. In this country, that is what is known as downsizing but in England, it's called being "made redundant." I like to be realistic and call it getting fired. In our example, this meant that the remaining unfortunates had the thrill of now contributing a sixty-hour agenda each week.

No one can "work" that many hours. In fact there is not a soul who could be at the office that long during the week and not get tired. It overwhelms me just considering the possibility. How do you think these two employees feel? However, let us look at these two workers and their reaction to their "promotion." The first week would result in a certain amount of productivity, but quite short of that sixty number requirement. After all, this goal means working ten hours a day for six days a week or twelve for five days. Either of these is nothing more than a killer schedule. Psychologically, they're off to a rough start.

By the time our two employees have finished for the week, they are rewarded with a one or two-day weekend where about the only thing they can do is rest. It wouldn't be enough time to get ready for the next week, so by the time Monday came around, each employee would probably not want to go full assault after the weekend. Each would need to have his batteries recharged, being somewhat burned out, resulting in a week of even less productivity. The cycle would continue with a few outcomes. First, less and less would be accomplished as the weeks wore on and each employee would be frazzled. Second, burnout would continue and proceed at an exponential pace, as would stress and health problems. Obviously, the company bottom line would suffer as much as those two workers, who may even wind up sick or in the hospital, or even worse.

I should mention a few words about burnout. This phenomenon occurs on a few levels: over a short period like a week as well as over the years. When I entered the computer world, someone related to me that burnout generally shows up there after about ten or twelve years. I was working a contract at Xerox in Rochester in 1986 when I felt the sting. If you have been paying attention and can do the mathematics, this prediction was right on the money – eleven years in my case.

In the treatise of our two workers under consideration, the burnout came almost immediately. Just thinking about the responsibility of sixty hours each week is enough to cause stress and concern. If either worker is hospitalized, it means someone else will have to be trained. That situation will involve a significant period of time and investment for the company and once a new candidate is hired, this same scenario of stress might play out. Even if neither individual has to miss work, you can see that projects just aren't getting done in the group.

Someone might say – probably a manager – that they can routinely do sixty-hour weekly gigs without any difficulty. Well, maybe they are at the office for that time, but I doubt that much gets done. I worked a ten-week contract in Orlando at Sea World for a workaholic who felt that fifty-hour weekly stints were nothing. He could do it, so why couldn't we? We all wound up putting in ten-hour days. Besides being at the office for that time, I also had a ninety-minute commute each way, so I was saddled – pun intended – with a thirteen-hour day. That meant that if it took me a half hour for shaving, showering and breakfast, starting work at 7 am meant I had to rise at 5 in the morning. Assuming they paid me for lunch or I didn't have to take it – I could eat at my desk while coding – I would be home by 6:30 in the evening. As you can see, that was a rather long day.

How did I do it? As I mentioned, the contract was about two months or so, so I psyched myself out. The first week wasn't bad and at the end of it I told myself I had nine weeks to go. I saw the light at the end of the tunnel and just kept going. Not having a contract for a couple months and needing to pay the mortgage was an incentive as well. Of course, if management used their heads for more than nose and earrings, they could have started the project a month earlier and let us work forty-hour weeks for three months or until the job was done. That approach would not cost the company a cent more and may even have saved a few bucks.

In other instances, I worked on projects that seemed to have no limit to the hours each week. In addition, I had over an hour commute each way on too many occasions. This made for really long days, which I could have done without. Besides the big bucks, the Y2K projects that I became involved in brought truly long hours from Monday to Friday. The good news for me on any of those projects was that since it was a contract, I would be doing it for a limited amount of time and it would eventually end. Had it become too much, I could always have given my two weeks notice. Health is so much more important than money any day.

The same thing can't be said for our two employees. They may not have the option to leave, although that may have been the best thing for them. The real solution to the problem that management should have seen is to have four people, each working a thirty-hour week. This idea will result in a host of benefits for employees and employer alike. There will be more productivity, happier and more rested workers. This proposal means everyone is putting in a six-hour day – what a change. Laborers won't experience that much stress, if any at all, and there shouldn't be any health problems to speak of.

No doubt, some head honcho will complain of costs as well as profits but I shouldn't have to bring home the point that our two workers alone almost brought the company to ruin – or at least the department – so that situation needs to be scrapped. It will cost more, but you need to spend money to make money, so what's the big deal? You will save a great deal of money because people won't be deserting the corporation or committing hara-kiri, saving the organization replacement costs and cleanup expenses on the premises. I worked at one company where an individual asked for a well-earned raise but she was turned down. She left and the company wound up spending more getting her replacement and training that new person than had they simply compensated this veteran for her past efforts with a much-deserved increase in pay. People in management sometimes do dumb things!

There are a few other things that can be done to make the company better. Students in high school wind up with at least two months vacation between school years – provided they don't attend summer school. For collegians, the break is closer to three months. However, following commencement day and with the arrival of a full time job, the graduate realizes that her vacation will turn out to be a mere two weeks. That could be a bit hard to accept. Granting each new employee at least a four-week vacation will change this. Simultaneously, those who have been with the company for some time shouldn't have to wait so long for increments in their vacation time. Many countries have implemented these ideas, very successfully. Happier workers make better, more productive employees. They won't need or want to look for other jobs, either. You don't need to spend a cent on any kind of study to come to that conclusion.

Other considerations by management to alleviate problems as well as increase efficiency on the job include telecommuting, the four-day workweek and true flex time. The first means less stress, less road rage and less gas used, a great boon to the planet. Environmentalists will be leaping for joy in the streets! (They may want to consider moving over to the grass – you know how some people drive.) The reason why working at home is not allowed too often is because management can't even control the help at the office, so how do you expect them to have a handle on the workers when they are away from the shop? Maybe the answer isn't to keep workers in the office.

These are all great ideas to make the company better and who can argue with that? Today, it seems that corporations care nothing about the earth, their products or the people they employ. Corporations in the past may have acted even less ethically. The only considerations seem to be the bottom line, the stockholders and the owners. For success, you really need only three things: a good product, customers and workers who make sure that the goods are available. Any creation that is toxic and dangerous, such as bombs and blue vinyl, isn't going to help the air, land, sea and people who work in the plant or the consumer. Thus the product needs to be safe and something that is desired. Without employees, the greatest gadget in the world is useless since it can't make it to the market. By concentrating on what is to be sold – goods or services – and the workers, there need be no concern for owners or shareholders as each will be satisfied. You may not even have to worry about the customers! With neither good product nor people behind the scenes, there can be no profit and the company will fail.

Let us say that a business is successful but management wants to improve matters. This can be done by hiring more help and making the product better or perhaps even adding some new items. Allowing the goods to become inferior or downsizing and outsourcing will only result in the demise of the company, or at least no betterment. This has been shown on too many occasions, as studies have pointed out. If the customers refuse to buy, the products will sit in the warehouse, but the shortage of workers will contribute to the end for the corporation if the product is worthwhile. Along the way to success, the owners may need to accept fewer profits overall, but they should accept the fact that less cash in their pockets is much better than none at all. After all, how many millions does one really need?

3

Minimum in every sense of the word

In the first chapter, I mentioned remuneration for work performed, so I need to spend some time on how people get paid. We are all aware of the hourly versus salaried employees, but there is another method of payment called "piecework." This involves getting paid by the amount of work you do. If you are employed on the farm with this system, you will get paid depending on the amount of vegetables you pick. For example, it might be one dollar a bushel.

As you might guess, this approach probably will only benefit management and it will be tough on the workers. Perhaps we should call it "piece on you work." I had a job one summer where I got paid by the number of grocery carts I picked up. I was given a truck – they paid for the gas – to drive and roam the neighborhood gathering baskets. I don't recall how much they paid me per cart – it may have been fifteen cents. As it turned out, I did quite well, making more per hour than when I was stocking shelves inside the store. Of course, I didn't stop for coffee breaks every hour. The bad news was that it only lasted for the summer.

Being salaried has advantages as well as drawbacks. It means you get the same pay each week – not a bad thing – but management will probably assume you can work fifty or sixty hours without a problem. Forty hours is only a starting point. If management has the idea that you are available and can work in excess of the minimum each week, I would only suggest that every so often a twenty or thirty-hour week for the employees should be acceptable to management, but I doubt that they will see it that way. I was salaried as a teacher as well as in my first job in the business world. For me, this worked out fine but unfortunately many employees become slaves, succumbing to the nazi leaders in the company.

Getting paid by the hour is another scenario, especially as a consultant. As a contractor, the paychecks are substantial but they don't compare to what those in upper management see or what those at Arthur Anderson once saw. On more than one occasion, I am sure that I got paid more than my supervisor, not including benefits, but then again, I did more work so it was justified. For the ordinary worker, the hourly wage is grossly inadequate – which seems to be the way more people in the work force are getting paid today. As I write this, the minimum wage hasn't been increased in close to a decade. If you factor in inflation, this means that the laborer has actually suffered a decrease in pay. If those in Congress can approve their own pay raise in the middle of the night, the least they can do is legislate a substantial increase in the minimum wage. It should go up to at least $15 an hour. I base this on one vast discrepancy between the pay of management and those who sweat to bring home too few dollars each week for their family. Over the years the gap has only widened and continues to do so.

With this proposed new hourly rate – which many in charge will dispute on the basis that it will bankrupt them – the worker will receive a yearly compensation of about $22,000, based on a thirty-hour workweek and 48 weeks of work. This is a huge improvement over the poverty level, which varies from state to state and also depends on the size of the household. The following chart is for the year 2005.

2005 HHS Poverty Guidelines

Persons in Family Unit	D.C. and 48 Contiguous States	Alaska	Hawaii
1	$ 9,570	$11,950	$11,010
2	12,830	16,030	14,760
3	16,090	20,110	18,510
4	19,350	24,190	22,260
5	22,610	28,270	26,010
6	25,870	32,350	29,760
7	29,130	36,430	33,510
8	32,390	40,510	37,260
for each additional person, add	3,260	4,080	3,750

With $15 as the new hourly pay, the yearly salary of the worker will increase for more than a thirty-hour workweek, but even for the shorter hours, it is still more than double the amount of $10,000, which is what the current minimum wage yields. The new salary amount is a huge improvement but it will still result in some struggles to run a household on the part of its recipients, especially for larger families. Nonetheless, it is a good start, and a great deal better than $5.15 an hour.

To counter those in management who insist that this increase may cause their company to go belly up, maybe their endeavor isn't supposed to succeed. I need only remind business proprietors that to make money, you need to spend it. Also, giving is much better than receiving, and greed is after all, one of the seven deadly sins. Stop dreaming of huge profits and think solely about making a living. The world will be a better place! Don't be like Enron – you know where that corporation is today. Revisit the idea of what makes a company profitable – I need not remind you that it's the workers and the product. If you can't accept that fact, you might just as well go out, find a job and not entertain thoughts about starting your own business.

It doesn't matter whether you are a small business or a huge congloomerate – if politicians can make up their own words, why can't writers? – treatment of the employees should be the same. To get the money to pay the help, you have a few options. First, there will have to be downsizing – of people in *management* who just don't earn their pay. You probably should weed out the dead wood in the office as well – those who sit around sleeping all day and those who don't produce, even while awake. Second, pay cuts will have to be made for those with exorbitant salaries in upper management. I've said it before, and I will say it once more, "How many millions do you really need?" Maybe a better question might ask, "How much can you spend?"

Throughout history, there have been moguls who amassed huge amounts of money by monopolizing an industry. This effort drove others out of business, resulting in huge unemployment for many people. A more pronounced effect was huge amounts of cash in the pockets of those with this squeezing process. Then, realizing that it was time to obtain a better image, these giants opened their wallets to help out the poor in their struggles. Of course, had they allowed their competitors to exist, their wallets wouldn't have been so fat, but simultaneously they wouldn't have needed to contribute to help a problem that they themselves created. It doesn't take much to realize that this horrendous practice is still with us in the twenty-first century.

It always annoys me when I hear a huge corporation complaining that it isn't making enough money. It was especially irritating during 2006 when gas prices went through the roof in the United States and the oil companies were accused of gas gouging. This came at the same time when these companies showed all-time record profits, while getting all kinds of tax write-offs. Maybe the cash from the register added up, but so did the conclusion that the people were getting stiffed at the pumps.

Unfortunately, energy companies aren't the only guilty parties in this day and age.

So we need to solve a few problems here. One is the difficulty facing corporations because their profits are down – yeah, right! – and the other has to do with payment to the workers. We need to address the huge disparity in pay between those who sign the paychecks and their employees. Perhaps it might be advantageous to look at a single company that isn't deficient in profits. That company is Wal-Mart. At the same time, the people who help make this corporation so highly profitable to shareholders get paid so little that they can't even afford to shop at the store where they work. The employees get no benefits such as insurance and they are deprived of the right to organize. Even more outrageous are the cases where workers have been instructed to keep working even after they had punched out. Maybe they should have landed some punches on their own.

Besides this travesty, the corporation is guilty of having no concern for the environment and it uses products that are created by citizens of the third world – who aren't paid anything close to the shameful minimum wage. Studies have shown that what is being sold in those stores is vastly inferior to what we expect of a business. Thanks to vast amounts of money spent on advertising, people still flock to these stores, which boast of the lowest prices in town. That might be true, but then the quality is also the lowest.

In the fall of 2006, Wal-Mart must have been feeling the heat since their image was suffering and the word was out on some of their practices. I didn't see the entire campaign but somehow I spotted an ad where they decided to emphasize Christmas rather than just the buying aspect of the holiday season. I'm not thrilled about political correctness, so if nothing has been done to address the social justice problems that I pointed out, this effort is nothing more than glossing over the real problem. Don't put halos on your heads if you don't deserve them.

The good news is that an organization can change. It can be more responsible and still survive. What's more, by acting with more concern, it can even reach higher gains in profits than currently are being recorded. If it doesn't change its policies and procedures, it can become extinct. That is because we the people have the power to affect change and send an important message. We can boycott MallWart and the result will be a different way of conducting business or the end of Sam Walton's empire. Education of the masses and people working together can bring this about.

This can be done with any corporation that has no concern for the consumer, worker or the planet. You might argue that people shop at Wal-Mart because of the prices. Doing a bit of calculating, it stands to reason that if the goods are garbage, the low prices don't make any of the products worth anyone's while, as I have already pointed out. Another way of getting around this dilemma of shopping there has to do with the realization by consumers that they can get by without making certain purchases from time to time. This should help free the buyers from having to rely on any one company in particular. From the people camping out and lining up before five a.m. on Black Friday, 2006, it appears that many people will discover higher credit card bills in the months to follow.

I emphasize again that if changes aren't made to a few concerns of social justice at the corporations, there is no guarantee of profitability. Having been a consultant at so many companies over the years, it never ceased to amaze me that the places where I put in time were still profitable despite some of the questionable business practices – some may have been immoral but others were just stupid and didn't make sense. The venues made money but that could have been increased so easily by incorporating ethical as well as good business practices. You may have heard about corporations that instead of recalling a deficient product, decide the cost of litigation to settle claims is less, and do not institute recalls. Why make any effort to get the product back and replace it? You may not want to use the individuals who came up with this choice as any kind of advisor or to defend you in court.

I can't emphasize enough that corporations have to use common sense in their business dealings. This recall / liability choice is absolutely insane because one huge lawsuit under these circumstances could result in jail time and the demise of the company. It seems that this available option is nothing more than Russian roulette or rolling the dice – but that is exactly what has and continues to be done in many instances. The same can be said of a polluter. Unfortunately, limits on frivolous lawsuits give people with money too much protection even though their own behavior is questionable. You may have heard that the corporation is now endowed with the rights of a citizen. Sadly, they don't feel that this privilege involves any responsibility.

I have always felt that a company that pollutes should pay for the cleanup and remediation. If someone at a bank robs the public of five million dollars, they should pay back at least that amount, be fined and serve time in jail for their crime besides. All too often these thieves have gotten away with this action and paid back only a fraction of what they stole. If they pilfered the cash, they must have it somewhere – maybe it's in their estates. Any decent judge would demand that these properties be used to pay for as much of the damages as possible. If you are going to be in prison for some time, the palatial estate won't be needed anyway. It is time to change the laws that protect the possessions of criminals from being used in settlements for crimes committed.

I close the chapter with a suggestion offered some years ago by the humorist, Art Buchwald. Since those in management – so grossly overpaid – really are only interested in the prestige, why not reverse their salaries with those of the janitor or housemaid. The management folks would still have their titles and plenty of power and those hourly workers would be great a deal happier. The minimum wage issue wouldn't be a concern anymore.

4

Make sure they have health insurance

Perhaps it is time to boot all the immigrants out of the country – illegal and otherwise, including their descendants. That would get rid of all the Bushes, Cheney, Delay, Foley, Cunningham, Kissinger, Gingrich, Rice, Perle, Rumsfeld, Limbaugher Cheese, Coulter, Wolfowitz and Rover – the other dogs can stay. Maybe that's a better idea than I thought! Nonetheless, it would leave only the Native Americans and there would be no one left to buy the cigarettes or flock to the casinos. That idea wouldn't fly.

Of course, that idea might cause a few problems with the Statue of Liberty. We could send it back to France for a credit – UPS and Fed-Ex could fight over the shipment – or replace the uplifted torch-bearing hand with an outstretched Nazi-like arm, begging people to turn back and go home. It might also be appropriate to change the words that beckon those fleeing persecution from foreign lands. The new words could be "Give me your tired, your poor – just as long as they have health insurance."

What wall will have to be built to keep out those from other nations? Will it be higher than the Berlin Wall or the recently erected wall between Israel and Palestine? The good news is that the construction will result in jobs. The Americans can work on the U.S. side and the immigrants – although then they wouldn't be – can labor on the other side. There has got to be a cost saving, there. Knowing our government, Halliburton will get the contract, subcontract out the work and overcharge for the job.

The problem is not an easy one but it really should not have existed. If the government and all its intelligence agencies couldn't stop a few terrorists, do you think that they will be able to hold back a few million immigrants? I think not. Besides, who will do the undesired, necessary jobs that others won't do?

The problem is complicated for other reasons. The government and the corporations simply haven't done their jobs. After all, don't we have an agency called the Immigration and Naturalization Service (INS)? There also are employers who think nothing of hiring people from other lands because they require so little in the way of remuneration and benefits. They can offer minimum pay or less, long hours and need not concern themselves with sick days, vacations, health coverage or injuries to the help. As a result we have a system that was supposed to have been eradicated by the Civil War. Slavery abounds if you look at the immigrants' situation, the plight of the middle class and poor as well as those working overseas for American companies or in Third World nations for even less pay. As it stands, the minimum wage will not allow anyone to survive in our society.

Perhaps the words *downsizing* and *outsourcing* need to be mentioned as well – it may be more appropriate to call them *job termination* and *shipping jobs overseas*. The real problem is not with the poor, the downtrodden and the rapidly diminishing middle class but with the union of the government and corporate America – neither of which could care less about the people. Their only concern is for power and greed, lining their pockets and those of their shareholders with green. At the same time the earth is losing out because of the environmental pollution, becoming brown – we all know what Brown did for New Orleans.

Firing people and moving jobs from an area only point out the fact that corporat America – Dan Quayle might have the "e" I need here – could care less about anything other than profits. I should throw in that some of the blame needs to be shared by the government because of the mess that they have allowed. I see many of these concerns in emails that people send me daily.

Some of this may be meaningful and I may even act on it, but on too many occasions people forward material without even considering what is being said. It's almost as though they see the word magenta in the correspondence and since that's their favorite color, they send the email on. One of the things school should have taught you was to do your homework first.

All of us in America are immigrants. We may have been born here but our parents, grandparents or their parents somewhere along the line came over to Ellis Island years ago to escape hardship and persecution and in order to have a better life. Actually, there are some people in this country who aren't immigrants, but most of their ancestors were massacred by the government and the rest sent to reservations. Joseph Marshall III tells of those Native Americans and their early struggles for survival in the Midwest in the nineteenth century in *The Journey of Crazy Horse: A Lakota History*. In reality, even the Lakota are immigrants because their ancestors made it to this hemisphere from other lands. Kicking all the immigrants out would leave us with no NFL season ticket holders.

People falsely claim that the immigrants take away American jobs. Actually, if you have been paying attention, the jobs have been shipped overseas – I've mentioned this new way of doing business enough times already. I returned from a trip east to Maine in September 2006 and I recall quite a few people who waited on me that probably weren't born here. If so, they had unusual accents and I'm not talking about southerners or people from Brooklyn, although I was at dinner one night where many of the guests were the former. The restaurant fed them because they brought money – big wads.

Another suggestion is that we need to build huge fences to keep out foreigners and this effort will restrain terrorists as well. Maybe the latter are already here. If not, they probably can climb over the wall. Will security at the airports have to start checking for ladders now? They have to check for those fold-up ones that you can put in your suitcase. Perhaps all this talk of terrorists is nothing more than a ploy to create fear. Creating fences is nothing more than a huge waste of resources that could be used elsewhere. Rather than spend money on keeping terrorists out, wouldn't it be more beneficial to make the effort to eliminate terrorism in the first place. Look at the root causes and not throw away money by doing really foolish things that just won't work.

As long as this country exists and other countries treat their citizens badly – that's putting it mildly – we will always have people trying to make a home here. The government's policies toward them needs to be changed so that immigrants who want to be United States citizens can do so, in a reasonable amount of time. If someone wants to visit this country, whether to get a job, go to school or just have a one night stay in the Lincoln bedroom at the White House, that should be allowed but also controlled so that the stay is limited within reason. I don't think that this is unreasonable. All right, maybe I went overboard with the Lincoln bedroom, but everyone needs her sleep.

More needs to be done for the work force and all this is connected to immigration, the minimum wage, health insurance, the workweek, downsizing, outsourcing, NAFTA, CAFTA, Fels Naptha and Kafka. It is about time that greed in its most obnoxious state is removed from the planet. I am referring to the gulf between the rich and the poor. We will always have both, but it's time to take some of those dollars from the affluent and give them to those in need. This process should result in few complaints from those at the top but will also cause the less fortunate to have better lives. It will improve the economy, result in less crime and have a huge part in eliminating insurrection, which many people feel is a huge imposition on their lives. Since the number of down and out seems to be increasing, we better not rule out the possibility of rebellion in some form – I will talk later about thresholds. The riches and resources are here. Why not use them to make a better society for all?

It amazes me that there is so much talk about unemployment and yet there is so much work to do. I need only mention New Orleans in the wake of Katrina, but that is only a start. If there is this need in areas of the country, then why do we have people not getting hired and working? Why are people having such a tough time finding work while others are putting in weeks of sixty hours or more? It does no good if the employment rate is one percent but a great majority of the work force is getting paid a scant five bucks an hour. That low rate is insignificant if a woman has to work three jobs or someone can't find work and it just isn't reflected in the employment numbers. Once again statistics are used to spin the truth – something that happens much too often.

People complain that there is no money and yet we are the richest nation on earth. Let's compromise and see what can be done about this problem. It is going to take a joint effort – who said marijuana can't be beneficial? – to achieve these goals. Government must pitch in, but corporate America has to contribute as well. Neither can do it alone. If a company refuses to allow unions on the premises, they should pay the workers a sufficient wage and treat the employees in such a manner that the latter will have no desire to organize. The only reason why unions were ever formed was because the companies had no concern for the worker and cared only about the bottom line.

The government has to work to solve the labor crisis and building electrified fortresses around any nation just isn't cost effective. Perhaps some laws should be changed, but I feel enforcing what already exists may do the trick. There also needs to be some government regulation so that criminal corporations become a thing of the past, even if we somehow allow for felonious corporations – for the short term. We need to get to a point where the construction of prisons is terminated – even though some are necessary for lawyers, lobbyists and politicians. This should be replaced with the building of more schools and improving those places of learning that already exist. You can spend a dollar for education or ten dollars or more for houses of detention. I would prefer my tax dollars to go to the former.

5

Pick your own cotton

I spent a small amount of time on the question of slavery in the book that I had published in July 2003. Abraham Lincoln may have been our greatest president because of his efforts in preserving the union as well as giving freedom to all. Many of us feel that the Civil War eradicated the peculiar institution. I don't agree.

How do you explain the need for the civil rights movement a century later? Why didn't women receive the right to vote in the nineteenth century and former slaves that same right until after the Civil War? There is little doubt that slavery still exists in our society today. Downsizing workers and making those left behind work sixty hour weeks is slavery just as is paying immigrant labor a pittance for performing dangerous work while the shareholders, owners and upper management of a corporation receive huge financial benefits. There is something drastically wrong when it takes a corporate executive a few months to "earn" what the average laborer will not see in a lifetime. It is even more abominable when these businessmen receive huge bonuses and stock options even though the company has a bad year. Why do CEOs get booted out the door with a huge retirement package? The plight of workers in Third World countries as well as citizens of this country who receive the minimum wage can't be anything but another example of slavery. The chapter title is another way of saying, "Take this job and shove it." Apparently some of the goals of the Civil War haven't been accomplished even today!

This merely points out that slavery is not gone from the planet. Exploitation exists in the same way it did a century and a half ago. Working conditions at the beginning of the new millennium are not much different than what occurred in the middle of the nineteenth century. The way individuals were treated then and the methods of today are only a bit different. If we compare society around the globe to the nineteenth century with all its evil labor practices, not much has really changed.

Slavery is prevalent when the minimum wage is $5.15 an hour. The labor unions would never have been created were it not for slavery. A woman working at a corporation on the weekend only indicates that the peculiar institution truly wasn't eradicated by the Civil War. Slavery hasn't been removed from our society when an individual has to work two or more jobs merely to stay above water, even if he is in pool maintenance. That nasty idea still exists if children get home from school before their parents every day and have to cook their own dinner.

Slavery is here if a person is well off and able to retire but instead stays at his present job and gets another part-time gig besides. This only eliminates an opportunity for someone else who really needs the income. Volunteering to help others is an entirely different story and to be commended. Slavery is still with us if people wait eight hours at the polls to vote, when they should be home having dinner after a long day at work. It is even worse if they get to the table to check in before voting but are denied that right because of some felony charge that applies to someone else with a similar name or because their skin is darker than the person at the polling place talking to them. As disgusting as that is, it doesn't quite compare to the vote that someone casts that doesn't get counted because a voting machine has been programmed to change the vote to the person from the party for whom the vote wasn't cast.

Slavery is around when someone who really dedicates himself to a company with his efforts is given a small buyout and a pen set as a gift of appreciation. At the same time, the president's daughter has her own office and continues her job – although not too many people know what she is doing at the company – she herself may not have a clue either. Slavery happens when people are put at risk by working in a coal mine or vinyl factory, where others are dying merely because all safety rules are violated.

Slavery is with us when the poor are told that their enlistment in the service will never send them into battle. These young people do it to escape poverty and crime and in order to get an education that they couldn't afford otherwise. Within a few months they are fighting the rich man's battle in a foreign, dangerous land.

Slavery is also encountered when people are addicted in some way. Human beings are slaves to their job, which sometimes results in the fact that they discover they can never retire. There are other unfortunates in the work place. How many times have you heard of someone's retirement followed shortly thereafter by that person dying? Recently I heard a few people of retirement age proclaim that they had no thought of retiring in the near future. Too many times I hear someone mention that she has a "good job," but I only feel that those two words are an oxymoron. Keeping in mind all that has been presented about the peculiar institution, it doesn't appear that many "good jobs" are around anywhere. I have mentioned many reasons why we hate work and obviously "slavery" is right up there as a cause.

Being a slave to your job could mean you're a workaholic. These people still make up a good part of the population, probably more so than when I finished my first book on work. In the early part of October 2006, I was at the Lighthouse Festival at Golden Hill State Park on Lake Ontario, trying to sell my books and raise a few dollars for the Lighthouse Fund. A gentleman came to the area where the authors were stationed and started perusing my book on work. I asked if he was a workaholic and mentioned that the book was ideal for that type of person. He didn't say much, so I added that the book makes a great gift, especially if you know some of those people – who doesn't? Well, he didn't buy the book or any of my others. I should have realized that he fit the profile of one who works too many hours as he had a beeper hooked onto his belt. I doubt that what I saw was a wide, rather short pocketknife.

I will get into my feelings about Sunday in a later chapter but for now I need to talk about those annoying cell phones, beepers and pagers. It is obvious that too many people have those gadgets. Carrying those things means you are a slave, as does the idea of 24/7, which is absurd. Once the thirty-hour workweek is implemented, the chains on our legs will at least be loosened or removed entirely. With any luck, the majority of us can survive by working a normal five-day week, with only a few of us reporting on the weekend.

Pagers won't be needed, except for a very small number of workers. However, to get to this point, a great deal needs to be done. It will take a Herculean effort on the part of management as well as on the workforce to accomplish this more accommodating workweek at the factory. My experience with computers only points out that not only can systems get better, but also they have to improve. Otherwise we will forever be stuck with sixty-hour weeks, which is not practical or feasible, since it doesn't work.

There is a huge correlation between improvements in the way things are done and how long the workweek is. By spending the time in development with some forethought, creating an error-free system means fewer people have to be on call. This approach is working smart, which is vastly superior to working hard, or becoming a slave. The smart choice means projects won't be rushed into production. The alternative could come back to bite the managers and employees alike in the area where there would prefer not being stung. Planning and effort will pay off as no one – worker or supervisor – wants to have to spend time working on a weekend when they could be shopping.

We have the opportunity to make things better and eliminate all those extra hours at the workplace and by doing so, the result will be an increase in productivity. A byproduct of this is a healthier workforce, which management won't complain about, and neither will we. The fewer hospital and doctor visits I have to make, the better. Technology has gotten to the point where there is no reason why these goals can't be reached. Unfortunately, what should have been a great tool to better employers and employees alike has only made a mess of corporate America and made us slaves. I'll get back to that problem later.

6

The more you spend, the more you save

A few sayings and ideas upset me because of their ridiculousness. I'm sure you've heard of *fighting for peace* or the idea of creating bombs as deterrents. I'm sure that someday – it probably has been done but I'm not aware of it – a book on pleonasms will be written. From my point of view, these ludicrous combinations of words and ideas are great because they give me more book ideas.

This chapter title fits into that same category. It doesn't take a genius to conclude that you are either spending cash or saving it – you can't do both at the same time. This is similar to the fact that you either are asleep or awake, although I've seen some people that I couldn't tell which state they were in. There is no way in the world that I can create a situation where my credit limit is reached and simultaneously I have more money in savings. You might insist that I never heard of the rebate that is offered with most credit cards. This has not escaped me but I have discovered that the small percent that you get in return is nothing when compared to your Visa or MasterCard bill. If you carry a balance, your bonus won't compare to the interest that you'll have to pay.

This title is certainly a flawed statement, but you see it everywhere. It would have been more accurate – and longer too – to call it, "The more you save and the less you spend, the sooner you can retire," or "The more you spend, the less can you save and the longer you will have to work." Some time ago, a friend of mine mentioned that an expenditure could be used as a deduction on my tax return. This person was right as I might have less of a tax burden, but at the same time I'd have less cash in my wallet because I spent it in this manner. This should be considered.

Shoppers justify their habits by using all kinds of tricks, such as rebates, refunds and coupons. They spend hours clipping the latter and more time sorting them out. In general it's a waste of time because they soon find that the coupon has expired, so it has to be tossed. On the other hand, if they use every last one that they clip, won't they be buying stuff that they don't really need? My philosophy is that if there is a coupon for something that you would buy anyway, why not save the coupon? You can see that sometimes a generic brand name might be available for less, even with a coupon for the name brand product. You could clip a coupon for a product, but never find a store that sells it, so once again, the coupon is worthless. These are all scams and I hate them, but if you want to retire sooner, sadly, you will have to use them.

Another way of getting money back is through one of two types of rebates. The first is an instant rebate where you get a reduction in the price of an object when you buy it. This by any other name is really a discount. This situation means that the company really wants to give you money back. The second type is a bit sleazier: the dreaded rebate by mail. I say that because it is the type of reimbursement that you may never see despite all your good intentions.

Suppose you buy a wood chipper like the one used in the movie *Fargo*, and there is a rebate advertised but the store is out of the rebate forms. You may never see any refund. Even if you do get the form, what if you forget to send it out? What happens if it gets lost in the mail going or coming? There is the possibility that the company offering the rebate won't give you your due even though you sent everything that was requested. Suppose that the offer has expired. In any of these cases the rebate will never reach your house.

In order to get this refund, I don't like the fact that you have to send the rebate form, register receipt and also proof of purchase, UPC code, bowling handicap and your last newborn. You would think that the form and receipt would verify that you indeed bought the product. Maybe the manufacturer doesn't really want you to get a refund. Why not have the rebate form inside the box and only require that you send it and the receipt? If companies are really serious about giving rebates, why don't they simply give instant rebates?

On one occasion I sent back all that was required for a fifty-dollar rebate – these are the ones that you want to send back and track. After a few weeks I was notified that I wasn't going to receive a cent back since I didn't include the box that the product came in. I had sent the receipt, form and proof of purchase, which they requested, but they didn't ask for all the packaging. For that amount of cash, I sent the box the software came in and in about four weeks, I got the fifty bucks. I won't say who ran the company with this promotion, but I will mention that his name rhymes with the name of the high school in the movie *Carrie* and the motel in the movie *Psycho*.

Some time ago I bought twelve quarts of motor oil for which a rebate was offered. That was in the days when I still changed the oil in my car, which I don't do anymore. I had to send the usual stuff back and the proof of purchase could be either from the case or from the individual quart containers. I wanted the case UPC code – it would have been easier – but the store only had single quarts of oil so I didn't have much choice. When I tried to remove the proof of purchase symbols, I had no luck even after soaking the containers in warm water for some time. Maybe I should have let it soak longer – like a few months! Eventually I just sent the form and register receipt. I am not sure if I ever did get that refund as they all take so long and we lose track. I am not one to have a separate coupon refund tracking file on my PC.

There is another difficulty with these rebates. The directions state that you should allow six to eight weeks for your refund. I've seen some that take even longer. I realize that Newman works for the post office – I believe Cliff Claven retired – so that may be a factor, but does it really have to take two months to get a rebate? Once again maybe the companies do not want to give you a refund.

Every so often I will see a case of beer advertised on sale for $12.99. That's the price you'll pay with the two-dollar rebate. The refund form will specify a limit of two refunds per family per year. Let's say that you need your daily six-pack fix. This means that if you already had your limit of refunds for the year, you won't get a rebate now. This then is a case of false advertising as well as alcoholic discrimination. But of course the sale with rebate is nothing more than an attempt to get you to buy the product in the first place. Rebates aren't typically meant to be paid out since manufacturers force you through the process rather than discounting the item to begin with. After all, why not save all the paperwork and costs involved for the company and eliminate all those refunds that have to go through the mail. That should be the way companies do business.

Whether we believe in rebates and coupons or not, the campaign is on to spend. It's been going on for years and with each passing day, I am convinced that people will buy an elephant if the price is minimal, or you can charge it, rather than the other way around. "But honey, I couldn't pass it up – the price was so low."

We get bombarded with confusing, dumb ads on television and radio every day – isn't commercial TV great? I only buy the newspaper on Sunday but the inserts for sales are never-ending. One of the first things I do is sort them out and get them into the bin for recycling. There actually is something they are good for, but it would have been more beneficial to the forest if they weren't produced at all.

We're also given the opportunity to delay payment by accepting an offer for a credit card with a limited time interest rate of zero percent. The fine print, which is hard to read, says that after six months, the percentage settles in at a comfortable

24%. That doesn't give me much comfort! That high rate can get even higher with any delinquency in payments. As I see it, that's highway robbery, but I need to talk about other bandits. These are the ones we need to beware of in the case of identity theft. Coincidentally, I think much of the blame for this way of sponging off hard-working people rests with the credit card companies. Their irresponsible junk mail winds up in the wrong hands and innocent people really suffer. Maybe they should be held accountable.

We see all kinds of credit card offers with low rates and rebates as well. The papers are full of ads as are our TV screens urging us to buy, even though we don't want or need these products. With all these great opportunities to not have to make payments for two years or more, how does one not go shopping? But after all, wasn't that a suggestion offered after the events of 9/11 by some president?

As a parent, you have a difficult enough task raising children. Add to that the fight you have with the kids after they implore you for some junk they saw advertised on the tube. How many times do you have to say no? This is followed by comments such as, "But Billy has a nucular reactor simulator," and "You don't love me." What can a mother do? It's not easy to find the answers, but you need to hold your ground and somehow get across the point that the family income is a bit short of that of the CEOs of Enron or Global Crossing. You can also add the good news that no one in the family is presently making license plates for a livelihood.

Because something comes down in price, people tend to justify their purchase. This is especially true of electronics. So it's necessary to upgrade that PC, even though it's only two years old. My computer – on which I am writing this – is over four years and still functioning. Granted my computer doesn't behave any way near the way I would like it and I'm not going back to a typewriter or pen, so I'm stuck. I could buy a brand new system tomorrow, but I'd have to pay for it eventually. If

I used my credit card, I'd have installment payments as well as the necessity of installing the thing, which would take some time to get the way I want it. Whatever that involves, these are hours that I refuse to spend. Many people don't feel the same way as I do, but they are the ones who won't be able to retire for some time because of their generous – perhaps a more appropriate word is frivolous – spending habits.

In order to make life easier, it will take some discipline in spending. From my love-hate relationships with grocery stores, you could correctly conclude that I would rather see the dentist than go shopping. That's not precisely true but I'm not thrilled about entering retail stores. Perhaps I just don't buy in to all the hype regarding spending and don't care for the frustration of going to purchase something – which I thought I needed – and returning with nothing. Also, if you head over to Sears – I surrendered my credit card there years ago – and don't make it to the register, you will have spent time there that could have been used doing something else. It's also possible that you could do time in the hoosegow by walking away without paying for some goods – you might save money but not time.

I will mention the delay philosophy in buying in chapter 7, which could keep your credit bills to a minimum. However, if you use that thinking in buying a quart of milk, the baby may cry more than you can stand and you may have to pour beer over your Cheerios. This idea can't be applied to every purchase, especially necessities. We also need to determine just exactly what those things really are. Some of the gadgets that people consider "necessary" weren't around ten years ago so it's lame to give them that designation. There are many new objects that fit that category of being needed, and as you may guess, one of those is the cell phone. Surveys have shown that more than half the population feels that the cell phone is one of the worst inventions ever. At the same time the majority of people admit that they couldn't live without them. I'm not suggesting that those who rely on this annoying communication tool jump off a skyscraper or tall mountain, but things would be a great deal quieter. Truthfully, our working lives and the length of our careers will be greatly affected by our ability to distinguish what is required for living and what is optional.

Our buying habits could be altered a bit when it comes time to buying gifts. This behavior is to be applauded for the generosity aspect but faulted when finances are concerned. I have seen too many cases where the gift isn't exactly what the recipient wanted. The first clue to disappointment are the words, "Oh, a tie-dye tie!" (That, by the way is a small exclamation point, very small.) Perhaps we give out too many gifts. I think it just might be the wrong gift and deciding what is the right one is the real challenge. If you have no concern for how much you dish out for presents, your future retirement will take longer to arrive since your financial situation is greatly affected.

In October 2006, I saw a headline on the Internet that said that half of the people admit to re-gifting, the practice of getting a gift and then passing it on to someone else as a gift. I should emphasize one word here that is meaningful and shouldn't be overlooked: admit. Each of us has seen this done, without exception and probably even have done it ourselves. There is good news, though. In the survey, it is not clear if the recipient just gave what she got to someone else because it didn't fit or she didn't like it. As far as I know, this passing on of goods only becomes "re-gifting" when wrapping paper is involved – in some cases a paper bag might qualify. The solution may be as simple as limiting gifts to food and drink, which will always be appreciated, unless you offer the recipient some stuffed raccoon tails. I'm not so sure about alcohol if someone is on the wagon. The last thing you want is to hit a bump and spill the precious contents of the bottle.

What used to be a religious holyday has evolved into a corporate holiday. I'm talking about Christmas. If you spend so much money on gifts during the glorious season that your credit card for the purchases isn't paid off until June, you went overboard and January and the months that follow won't be that joyful for you. Keep in mind the re-gifting possibilities and limit your offering to something more significant. The holiday season should be a season of caring, but you also need to have concern for paying off debt as well. Remember that love is not equated to how much you spend on an item. A few more very good suggestions in this regard are desired lists, maximum spending per gift and the idea of asking for nothing at all. You could suggest a gift to some worthwhile cause instead.

7

Moving garage sales

If you read my book on missing intelligence, *for seeing eye dogs only*, you have a good idea of the humor in the title of this chapter, which is also related to the discussion on work. The third and last thing that bothers me has to do with yard sales, flea markets and moving. Once you move to a bigger house, someone comes up with the brilliant idea of a garage sale. This possibility is offered because it means less to pack but the move is dictated because you've run out of room in the house in which you live. I thank George Carlin for that insight. This "step up" implies the dreaded "moving day," which really involves much more time that a single twenty-four hour period. Actually, a transfer from one house to another may not be accomplished for many months, depending on the amount of stuff you own. I'm sure you know people who moved five years ago and still aren't completely unpacked.

Moving, flea markets and yard sales are intertwined and inevitable in our society. I try to avoid garage sales at all costs. I'm not happy moving either, although I will help others when they are involved in that adventure, provided I get paid with food afterwards and I don't have to do any packing. If I have to put things in boxes, I will probably throw away a great deal of stuff, so I won't have to worry about it. The people involved may never invite me to help them move again – actually, that might be a great thing.

The first few times I left one home for another, it was done with my car and there was a single trip. My vehicle was a small 1964 4-cylinder Chevy Nova, but it was sufficient enough to transport my books, clothes, stereo, records and other personal stuff in one move. This is how all these U-haul moments should be! Unfortunately, as we accumulate goods, it's not quite that simple. I have had a few adventures in moving, as I am sure you have had as well. Those are times that we have no desire to revisit.

Today, you see a preponderance of small buildings that give anyone the opportunity to have "self-storage." The reason for all these areas has to do with materialism, which is also the main reason for flea markets and marvelous moving moments. I might mention here an ad that I see almost daily when I try to get my email. It states, "You can get a $200,000 mortgage for $700 a month." Since you have too much stuff and now need to move to a bigger home, you also have the chance for a super-sized monthly payment and your name may not even be McDonald! The bank has a fair-sized interest in your house. They actually are the real property owners, except for a closet that's yours.

The yard sale, moving, big mortgage and materialism are all tied into work and somehow it seems that we have come full circle. Someone gets a raise and splurges on a high definition television. The purchase is paid through a credit card since the pay increase will be arriving in a few weeks. Since the boob tube is the great American wasteland, there probably was a better option: put the extra cash from the promotion away for the future or pay off a credit card. Since neither option was exercised, not only will retirement not be here at the scheduled time, it probably will be delayed even further because of this trip to Circuit City.

It appears that this employee didn't check his financial work sheet and instead went overboard. One of the problems with credit cards is that you usually have to pay for what you bought. It could take weeks, but eventually the bill will come due. The unfortunate reality is that all too often, a few small charges add up so fast to a large, unexpected payment. This is precisely why there are so many bankruptcies.

The desire to buy and buy – from a flea market or Macy's – eventually results in saying bye-bye to an early retirement. It is also a factor in saying good-bye to neighbors since moving becomes a necessity rather than an option. A better alternative is to buy without a credit card, using only cash. That way, if you don't have the bucks, you'll accomplish a few things. First, you won't be forced to buy a new home because your big screen television doesn't fit in any of your rooms and second, the product may not come home with you, meaning you'll need fuhrer yard sales (those are the ones run by Nazis in which people can't leave without buying.)

Granted, you can always shop for the best prices, but if you buy, you will still have stuff. Much of this you really don't need. I moved at the end of November 2003 and I have junk in storage in the basement that I haven't used since before that wonderful Allied Van Lines weekend. If you have something that you haven't used in five years, I can say with absolute certainty that you don't need it and can sell, give away or trash, unless it's a collectible or you are keeping it for sentimental value. If there is an item that you haven't used in two years, you may want to use the same approach to downsizing. Who said that was always a bad thing?

Let's return to this subject of bargain hunting for a moment. This is why people go to flea markets but then they have their own, and sell the same crap that they picked up at someone else's swap shop. It's an endless cycle and keeps the economy going – small time. I recall a sign of years ago that said, "We buy junk, sell antiques." I'd like to think that the progression goes just the opposite way. In reality, everything eventually deteriorates and turns into trash. The house you own today hardly compares to the brand new Cape Cod that you had built twenty years ago. To keep it up, you need to spend time and money, which brings us back to our subject, "work."

The people who brag about how much cash they saved are the same individuals who visit three supermarkets – there's that nasty word again – to get the "best prices." They saved $4 in the process but fail to tell you that they had to spend $5 in extra gas to do it. In any endeavor to save bucks, remember that time should be considered as well. You've heard of the guy who tried to do his own plumbing to save $50 but wound up with embarrassment as well as paying three times the amount he anticipated it would cost him to do it himself because his basement wound up with a pool. That was supposed to be the project for next year, but outside!

Many things are needed in our lives, but too many are really quite optional. Yet, we buy them anyway and they just sit around collecting dust. Each of these purchases means we will have to spend extra time at work to account for our high credit card balance. Maybe we should have a new attitude about buying things: when going out for the first time for this product, convince yourself that there will be no purchase that day. If you want the object, you will have to return to get it. This should give you plenty of time to consider whether you should open up your wallet for this stuff. This is the delay philosophy in buying option, which really works.

We should also consider the effect our spending has on the planet. The more we buy, the more we toss out and the more stuff there is in the landfills. In addition, everything on sale requires resources from the earth to produce. One thing we don't want is the possibility that something can't be produced because what makes it up can't be found anywhere. This does not even consider toxicity or pollution that our credit cards are doing to the air, land and water – for example the purchase of electronics products, which shouldn't just be tossed into landfills but properly recycled.

8

Show me where the money went

I mentioned the work sheet earlier to see how much you are spending, so let me spend some time on what I use. I have no formal training in financial planning but I have used a bit of common sense when it comes to the future. That may be why I retired from consulting at the end of 2001 – besides other factors, such as the fact that I had more than enough of my share of corporotten America. Perhaps my college studies had a bit to do with this decision as well. I did learn a few things in college in the sixties.

One idea that may be past its prime but really shouldn't be is saving, even when it appears that it can't be done. If you are making a hundred dollars a week and put aside a few dollars for the future, it can have a great impact on when you can retire, no matter how little you put away. You can refer to the examples in my other book on work for exactly what compound interest can do for you. In that book, I relate the tale of two individuals who each start an Individual Retirement Account (IRA), but their approaches are a bit different from each other. The results may surprise you. It's so amazing that it might entice you to start putting bucks away – and I don't mean in a mattress. You don't even have to like math.

Start with a simple savings account – although that will probably pay you less than one half a percent interest. If you look around for other possibilities, you should be able to improve on that disgustingly low rate. You might get lucky and find a credit union that will give you two percent interest for a checking account or a bank could offer you a savings account that pays that rate. However, you shouldn't stop there. As cash accumulates in this account, start moving some of it from the low paying account into either a CD or a mutual fund. The former has some limits, no matter which bank is involved, but you may be fortunate to find one with a four percent return on your investment.

A mutual fund should help your money grow faster, but it could also tank and you could be stuck with squat – and then you wouldn't be able to stand up straight. Seriously, CDs are secure but for your money to grow, not without risk, invest in a mutual fund. Your research may give you an opportunity for fair growth with minimum risk, but remember the greatest growth comes with more risk. Investing in the markets is to be considered but even taking cash from your bank to invest in a certificate of deposit is an improvement over an account that offers little or no interest.

You may be fortunate to find a mutual fund that requires a grand or less to start, but then you can add a small amount each month, like say $20. Maybe you'll have to put in $50 every thirty days, but that's only a bit over $12 a week. The best part could be that the investment can be transferred automatically each month from your checking account, so you will hardly notice that the money is gone. You'll have a pleasant surprise later. Of course, you should be aware of the ritual movement so that you don't bounce any checks. Obtaining ten dollars in interest while paying a fifteen-dollar overdraft fee doesn't help your future at all.

I mentioned earlier that you should put cash away even if you don't have it and that might sound contradictory. It's not as farfetched as you might imagine. A few years ago the IRA – not to be confused with the terrorist group that made amends – was introduced for those looking to the future. Some people felt that they didn't have the bucks to put two grand into this investment. However, they may have been able to get a loan for the money and somehow pay that off in a year or so, a piece at a time. What this initiative did was twofold: there was some saving done – even if it appeared to be minimal – and the interest on the loan may have been deductible on one's tax return. Besides that, the two grand could have been used on the return to lower the amount of tax for that year, since taxable income would have been reduced. If there was a tax refund, it could then be used to pay down some of the loan that was originally taken out. Why would someone ignore this great opportunity?

You might still complain that you couldn't get the loan because of a cash flow problem. It's really incredible how fast the bucks flow out the door. As they say, if your debits outweigh your credits, your assets in trouble. Who said you can't get past the censor? The real problem seems to be keeping expenses down. With inflation, that isn't easy.

Not long ago I developed a simple EXCEL spreadsheet to track expenses. It won't mean you'll have more cash but rather that you'll be able to see what is causing your dough departure. There will be certain costs that you won't be able to do anything about but others could be modified. That is a start. What follows is a sample of what the spreadsheet looks like. Note that you will only see half a year here because of space limitations. In your case, you can include all twelve months since EXCEL files are unlimited in both directions.

	A	B	C	D	E	F	G
1		JAN	FEB	MAR	APR	MAY	JUN
2	groceries	334.28					
3	heating	44.47					
4	car	28.60					
5	charity	36.95					
6	laundry	6.25					
7	Medical	165.73					
8	phone	24.10					
9	cable	8.23					
10	electric	40.40					
11	dinner	273.96					
12							
13	total	962.97					
14	income	1100.00					
15	what's left	137.03					
16							
17	groceries	14.87	6.98				21.85
18	dinner	50.35	21.00				71.35
19	laundry	2.50	3.75				6.25

Note that you can add fields to the spreadsheet and delete them as applicable. If you don't have cable or simply don't pay for it – don't worry, I won't report you – but have to pay rent, replace the "cable" row with one for "rent." A feature that I like is the SUM feature for the columns and rows. I merely put the numbers into the cells and the totals are calculated, once I set up that feature. To get the totals for January, select all the elements in the column, including the cell where you want the total to appear. In the case above, you would have selected twelve cells down the column, skipping the one with the heading for months. Then click on the AutoSum icon on the standard tool bar. You can do this for any total you want, whether horizontally or vertically.

Note that I went one step further by putting in "income" into the cell below the "total" and did a further calculation to see what money was left after expenses. This is the field "what's left" and the calculation is done by a formula, but it's quite easy. Note that in the example above, each row in the spreadsheet has a label (from 1 to 19), as does each column (from A to G). You can find these letters and numbers on every spreadsheet – in fact, every other entry is what I input, such as fields like "MAR" and "groceries." To calculate "what's left," we have to subtract expenses (our "total") from "income." This is done by selecting the cell in which we want this value to appear – here it is B15 – and then proceeding to the formula bar, where we place the formula, = B14-B13.

The field B14 represents column B and row 14, which is "income" while B13 stands for column B and row 13, which happens to be the "total," or our expenses. Don't forget the = sign. This formula just does the subtraction that you want and the result shows that you will be eating a lot of macaroni and cheese that week. This spreadsheet should make you realize that maybe you need to buy a few less clothes or not eat out at fancy restaurants that often. These are some things that can be controlled and the result will be more cash to put away for retirement. This should help to limit some of your spending. One of the other things that this spreadsheet does is make you realize how much you spend and how fast the money goes.

You might note that I have three rows beneath the "what's left" row. I use these to do intermediate calculations during the month. This is useful since I shop for meat and vegetables more than once a month so I can keep track as I purchase my Fritos from week to week. Most likely I do the laundry a few times, as well as head out to restaurants at least a couple times a month. As I enter these values, I get a running total in G17, G18 and G19. When I update the numbers for the month, I use the values in those three fields and then simply clear out these working fields and start over for the next month.

EXCEL gives you all kinds of possibilities for calculations and you can experiment with the tool bars. I created an EXCEL spreadsheet that allows you to key in a date in MM/DD/YYYY format and it gives you the day of the week as well as the Julian date. It also works in reverse and the procedure to do all this is a bit complicated but it shows that you can do quite a bit with a single EXCEL file.

You can take and use this information in another way. Let us say that you decide to cut down the amount you spend for groceries each month. You could simply decide on your limit for the month and then figure what you have each week to spend, which you can put into an envelope for that purpose. When the bucks are gone, you need to wait until next week before proceeding to the grocery store. Since you can live for days without food – there's probably stuff in your freezer and pantry as well – you should be all right, but you will need water, which isn't free anymore.

Obviously, you may not be able to reduce such bills as real estate taxes or gas and electric, but even those utility costs might be reduced slightly by a bit of conservation and not having all the lights on in the apartment. With a bit of creativity, you may be able to find a few dollars in savings here and there and it may not seem like much, but little by little these small amounts add up. That should be quite obvious if you look at your credit card and see that your bill is higher than you expected after spending ten dollars here and twenty there.

9

A fence that's needed but different

That fence I talked about earlier is a great example of pork – I'm not sure, but I don't believe any pig will be harmed in the construction of that divider. There are times when barriers are necessary. When I bought my house in East Aurora, I realized that the back yard was perfect for a garden. There was enough sun but I would have to prepare the ground. I borrowed my dad's rototiller and got moving on preparing the soil. There was another problem. If I didn't take some action, my vegetables would never make it into my kitchen as I had furry friends: rabbits, raccoons, deer and woodchucks. That's where the fence came in.

I bought sixty feet of fencing and then had to decide on a configuration. I could have had a 1 X 29, 10 X 20 or possibly 15 X 15 enclosed area. Instead, I chose to have a circular area – or something close to it. They say, "Once a teacher, always a teacher," and I'm no exception. For those of you who skipped geometry class or didn't quite comprehend the lesson, here comes a practical treatise.

The first three possibilities are rectangles, whose area is calculated by multiplying the length times the width. This exercise gives us three areas of 29, 200 and 225 square feet respectively. To get the area of the circle, we simply multiply the radius by itself times pi, which is approximately 3.14. We could create the circle, measure the diameter and then take half of it to get the radius. We could also solve the equation,

C = pi times d, where C is the circumference (in this case it's 60) and d is the diameter. Dividing d by 2 would then give us the radius. Solving the equation 60 = 3.14 X d is done by dividing both sides of the equation by 3.14 and thus d is about 19.1 and hence the radius is half of that or 9.5. Multiplying 9.5 by itself and then by 3.14 gives us over 283 square feet, a bit more than even the 15 by 15 plot. This choice has maximized the area for the fencing I bought.

You might say that this garden possibility will create problems for the rows of vegetables since some will need to be quite short. For us it won't be a concern because we won't be using conventional rows but instead will take advantage of what is called the postage stamp garden. This results in areas of produce here and there rather than rows. We should also worry about vegetable conflicts – the beets won't hit the tomatoes over the head but some vegetables shouldn't be next to others while a given herb and vegetable in close proximity benefits the growth of both. Botanists have figured this all out and we'll let it go at that.

Another thing that I will do is to plant the cucumbers along the fence and allow them to crawl up it. This will accomplish a few things. These plants spread out and doing this will save us space for other crops. The plants will be easier to maintain since weeds don't generally grow on fences and there is no need to worry about clumsy farmers stepping on the vines and killing off the vegetable. In addition, the cucumbers will be easier to see when they are ready to be harvested.

The postage stamp garden needs less weeding, which no one will complain about. I mentioned the following idea before in another book, but it's worth repeating. One innovative farmer came up with an ingenious way of farming and it helps to prevent other problems. He planted without plowing the entire land but rather by inserting the seed within the soil as he tilled a small strip of land. This made a lot of sense and points out the fact that weeding a garden may be way overrated. The wind can do a great deal of damage as the dust storms of the past have illustrated. Why increase this risk by laying the land bare?

As you can see, my gardening adventures used a new way of thinking and the results were very impressive. The farmer of yesterday worked hard, but I prefer to save time and energy by working smart. In my yard in East Aurora, I still had work to do and difficulties could arise, but that didn't stand in my way. For example, I couldn't get around the raccoons since they climb fences. I couldn't grow corn so I bought it from the farmer. Rabbits can fit through the small gaps in chain link fences but I foiled them with chicken wire. You could say that I solved even those problems and we can do the same in all issues of work and what goes with it.

I stated earlier that people don't have decent work and yet the help wanted signs abound, without getting answered while there are jobs that need to be done. Of course, some people are employed with jobs that pay well, so statistics don't matter to them. That can change when they are booted out of a company. There are some people who feel that they are indispensable to a corporation. If a person happens to get run over by a Mr. Softee truck – maybe that name should be changed here, since it is inappropriate if you are on the receiving end – the company will still be in operation whether that individual is hospitalized or never in need of social security payments.

I have met individuals who were so secretive about their work because they felt that this approach resulted in job security. Every one of us can be replaced, even people with specific skills. I once worked with some consultants who were completely versed in a particular software product. As a result, their hourly rate was extremely high – I thought it was obscene, but that's me. Unfortunately, if a few corporations decide to trash this software package and get another, it would leave these people without a contract. They still have to buy groceries – oh no, not again.

Having consulted at companies from New York to Massachusetts to Florida, I had a vast range of applications to work on and different computers as well. This meant it was never boring. I got to know quite a few different contractors, some of whom will make great characters in my next novel. In general, the consultants I worked with over the years were good people who really performed and deserved their high billing rates. Don't forget they had to pay for their own health insurance and still had to worry about putting groceries on their table and paying the mortgage.

You may have heard a lot about overpriced consultants. In the information technology business, our pay was decent, but nothing when compared to that of lawyers or agents. My philosophy was to never get caught sleeping at my desk – it sends the wrong message. I have always felt that the right approach is to do the best job you can, even finishing the task ahead of schedule. This effort should result in your contract being extended. Unfortunately, from my experience, you probably will be dismissed instead because your job is done ahead of schedule. Who ever said life was fair?

Strange as this sounds, some contractors figure that if they are hired for a six-month period, they will make sure that they don't finish too quickly. They don't want their stay at the company to end too soon, so they work in slow motion and stop action. You have to blame management for this scenario. In my opinion, if I am a manager, people who work for me and show initiative, finishing ahead of time, are the ones that I want there, even if not permanently, rather than those who milk the project for all it's worth. That is one of the problems with corpareate – as in a potato peeler – America.

Another occurrence I have already mentioned: getting rid of good people and letting the chaff stay on board. To me, it seems as though the best people always depart the corporation while the dead heads remain – nothing personal, Jerry! Company managers don't seem to discriminate as they apply the same policies to the full-time help as to the consultants. You can read more about how much I love management in the chapter, "BOSS spelled backwards is double SOB" in *Tick Tock, Don't Stop*.

In that same book, I described some of my consulting experiences, which should give you a few laughs. There were times for me as a contractor when things were hectic, but I can say that a few times I went to the think tank to do some serious reading. Your boss should give you assignments, and you shouldn't have to ask her. He shouldn't ever say, "look busy," which is one of the simplest things in the world for someone to do with a computer terminal, especially if you have Internet access. You'd be surprised how many penny stocks you can buy online. You can increase your portfolio, but it doesn't mean you'll accomplish anything other than getting closer to the five o'clock hour. Just make sure you pick good ones because you will need some cash if you get caught trading on company time.

I hated instances when I had no assignment or when I had to wait for a user to get back to me. If a project leader has nothing for me to do, why can't I go home, but still get paid? I can "look busy" there just as easily as at my desk. The food's better too. It seems that on most occasions, I had no difficulty making deadlines and was usually ahead of schedule. I do recall one assignment where I was straddled with two software systems that I didn't know that well, so I had to master them on my own. This prospect slowed me down somewhat, but I did manage anyway. Conversely, on another occasion, I was at a company where I didn't know their software, but I figured it out and by the end of the first day there, I had written an interactive program – one that uses a computer terminal to enter data.

Once you get some background in a subject – this applies to areas other than computers – you should be able to adapt and be successful no matter what you are called upon to do. There may be a struggle at first, but eventually you should do fine and you will get better at it with each passing day. This means people should praise your work and you should get raises ahead of time, or contract extensions. You also shouldn't have any concerns about job security – note I use the word, "shouldn't." Even if they boot you out the door for something, you should be able to move on to a better opportunity.

You really can't go too far wrong by doing your best. With that attitude, you may come to agree with my feelings about tasks in general. I thought that for most work that someone said would take me a week, I could finish it in less time. To me, it seems that somehow people are goofing off on the job. Making the effort will pay off, most of the time. You have to allow for the craziness in the corporations today for the exceptions that occur.

Since I mentioned "character consultants" earlier, you probably realize that there are full-time people who aren't much different from these high-paid traveling medicine show freaks. I taught a class in COBOL programming – many thought that this language would be obsolete before the end of the twentieth century, but it endures. One of my "students" wanted to finish the course but all he cared for was a job where he did as little as possible, if anything. He didn't want his effort to get in the way of a paycheck. I don't have to mention his name and I won't, but he is not alone with his dreams. I recall a project team meeting on my last contract where my boss mentioned some individual who had some position with the corporation, but few people knew what his work involved. I may sound like I'm repeating myself but this scenario happens day after day. The worst part is that it is allowed to take place.

If you haven't read *The Peter Principle* by Laurence J. Peter and Raymond Hull, I highly recommend it. It's an entertaining read but also a warning about what does happen in the work place. Simply stated, people rise to their level of incompetence. They have a job and are very good at it, but then get promoted and they fail in a big way. This is not true of everyone – just most of the population – but it's hard to overcome.

Suppose that Pat is a teacher, who after a time, does so well that raises come along as expected. However, Pat isn't quite satisfied and realizes that becoming a counselor could bring with it more remuneration. That is all well and good, but suppose that Pat gets this promotion but somehow doesn't quite live up to the task – great teacher, lousy counselor. This is a perfect illustration of the Peter Principle. It happens with defensive coordinators who get promoted to head coach but somehow get fired within a few seasons. Their team had the best defense in the league when they were in charge, but victories were scarce when these individuals became head coaches.

With some effort on the part of a worker, there is no reason why this scene has to play out, as the person could do just as good a job after being promoted as in his first assignment, or even better. This will help corparrot America – this is made up of the people who do and say everything their boss wants to hear. On the other hand, I have been involved with some people who were incompetent no matter what they did. I'm not sure anything could be done to help them. Still, they needed cash to pay the bills. Maybe, they just needed to try harder and concentrate. Even the person I mentioned earlier who was lazy can be saved and made into a productive member of the work force. It won't be easy but the choice can't be made by anyone other than he himself.

There was an incompetent individual that took my assignment on one contract and I described him in my book on work. He didn't fit the pattern of a competent consultant, but perhaps it wasn't entirely his fault. Now that I think of it, I replaced another individual on a different project that I mentioned earlier. I had a contract to do the programming for the order entry system I designed at Nestle Foods. The guy who I took over for mentioned to me that the work was about ninety percent done. From looking at his efforts, it appeared he was bit off in his estimate. That was the percentage that had to be done at that point, not the other way around.

This is the type of individual who gets into a corporation based on a false resume but somehow is never discovered to be a fraud. He leaves before anyone catches on to his charade. He then winds up either in a different department or at some other corporation and continues doing the same stuff, leaving once more before anyone is the wiser. This goes on for a few assignments, but how management doesn't figure out that he is as worthless as a phone that is missing the "5" is beyond me – you can still call some of your friends and be on the receiving end. However, this employee soon has a reputation, but more importantly, enough resources to retire. You might say this sounds like a government job but it can happen in the corporate world as well. I don't advocate this approach in any way.

10

I'm quitting schule for this job

The title of the chapter should be a good reason why a student shouldn't give up one desk for another at a corporation, no matter how high the salary. I have to thank the brilliant comedian Gallagher for that word *schule*, which my version of spellchecker has flagged. I saw the skit he did on spelling on the *Tonight Show* some years ago and it was hysterical, but brilliant. He also mentioned some of his skool experiences and used different words to point out why English is such a difficult language. The comedian has more intelligence in his little toe than the composite total smarts at some of the business meetings that I stayed away from.

I need not bring up various studies that show that in most cases, one's fortunes over a lifetime increase with formal education. A high school graduate will do better financially than a dropout but not quite as well as a college graduate. I'm not sure of what effect "Sumo come laudy" has on early retirement. I also don't feel that attending Harvard or Yale is any more beneficial than going to a college that costs infinitely less and is not as well known. In the long run, what counts is a degree or two. Attending a prestigious school will only mean that after commencement, you will have to make payments longer than if you settle for a degree from a state university, even if you were awarded a partial scholarship.

A professor once mentioned three words to describe grades in school: arbitrary, meaningless and final. He had it right except for one college grade that I received which turned out to not be final after all. I had it changed. That was an exception and certainly the mark we get for a course seems to be insignificant and quite random. You need only consider a structure where students are rated with these possibilities for grades: A+, A, A-, B+, and so on. What exactly is the difference between an A- and a B+? Is there a difference? Does it really matter? I don't think so. It's even worse when teachers grade on a curve, which only pitchers in baseball should be concerned with.

What counts is the education that takes place. My undergraduate professors didn't use the plus and minuses but we still could get A, B, C, D or an F for a course. I thought that the system at the School of Advanced Technology at Binghamton University was far more meaningful. It went way beyond even pass / fail. We could either pass the course or it was as though we never registered for the course. Since most of us paid for the classes ourselves – although it was much cheaper than what you'll pay today – we made it a point to not be in a situation where we shelled out cash for Advanced Bomb Design even though we didn't register for the session!

A teacher's job is to get the material across to the students. Of course, the students have responsibilities as well. Together, both can be successful. It won't be easy if much of class time is spent with tests, week in and week out. The degree program in computer science I enrolled in at Binghamton University was new, so I wound up with a grand total of one (1) test throughout the entire program. The nerve of that teacher! We did have to show competency by passing tests for six foundations courses before getting into the program, though. I did get my degree there, and seemed to get enough promotions as a programmer analyst and systems analyst and did well as a software consultant to indicate that the course was successful. What more can you expect from a degree program?

The aim of education is to do just what the aforementioned program achieved, at least for me. My fellow students there weren't slouches either. Nevertheless, some professors who are well paid feel a bit differently. They grade their students based on what they give back to them for a course, rather than the understanding of concepts. Puppets are fine for ventriloquists but not for the classroom. It may be difficult for instructors to make some determination relative to grades but that's what they are paid to do. Assigning huge amounts of homework and papers can only get in the way of learning. Obviously, each is required and it is up to the teacher to balance what is handed out. She needs to be aware that she isn't the only one giving out assignments. If a student is only taking one course, the professor should keep in mind that the pupil probably has a full time job during the day, so six hours of homework nightly is unreasonable. This applies in high school as well as at the university.

It might appear that the educational system is broken. Ethics don't appear to be that important as various scandals in the business world and politics can attest to. The Foley fiasco of late 2006 might indicate that the Republicans don't want your contribution. Instead, they want your first born! In this and a few other instances, ethics apparently were tossed out the window, but isn't that part of the learning process? Without principles, how can any society endure? When you see business documents loaded with spelling, punctuation and grammar errors along with incomplete sentences and misstatements of facts, one can only conclude that the educational system is in serious crisis. It needs changing all the way from first grade to graduate school. Kindergarten might be fine. I really don't know since I started with first grade – some people are smarter than others.

Another indication of failure has to do with costs, which I alluded to above. (Why end a sentence with a preposition when you can end it with two?) Today's costs for getting a degree are outrageous, obscene and unaffordable for most people. Since learning is so important, this needs to be changed. School needs to be available for everyone, no matter who they are. It should also not be so restricted that the only way individuals can get an education is by enlisting in the Army or Navy. The only possibility here is lowering the tuition fees and especially the cost of all that goes with it. College education should be free and subsidized by the government. This is a no brainer. After all, there is no better investment than in our youth and what is more beneficial than learning? Get the funds and get the program going!

This drastic change will give opportunities to all and save money in the long run. There will have to be some changes in the structure of the system as well. I have already made a few suggestions but you can see that incompetent teachers have to be weeded out of the system, which won't be able to support them. The whole testing experiment needs revamping since it is an endeavor that just hasn't worked. I apologize for not having all the answers, but I'm an idea person. Since what we have now needs a huge overhaul, we need to start somewhere.

My first real job was teaching mathematics in high school. Throughout those years, I noticed that people in the profession could come up against quite a few pitfalls. You could have one "challenging" student in a single class and that might drain all your strength for the day. The result could be that you shortchanged the others in the class. Even if you were fortunate to avoid that discipline problem, you may have had teachers in your department who weren't much help to you, were simply annoying or should have gone on Survivor – and not gotten booted off the island, ever. As a teacher, you could wind up with a department chairman who you wished was beamed up somewhere. It would be worse if he appeared to be supportive of all you did but then failed to come to your defense when you needed it.

An uncooperative principal, vice principal or board of education could be enough to lead you to get another assignment. Parents also play a huge role in your success. If they support you and really are concerned about their son and daughter, your task will be easier. On the other hand, if they take the side of their child instead of yours in some matter, you'll be up against a wall. You could also have a board of education that doesn't support you or principal, department head or close co-workers who make your life difficult rather than helping you in times of need. Note that a single one of these relationships could be enough to make you leave the teaching profession, so you will have a few challenges.

Any teacher can face all these possibilities when she embarks on a career in the world of education, and they happen at all levels of instruction, from Kindergarten to graduate school. What has to be done is minimize these conflict potentialities. This will only mean that school has to be a cooperative endeavor, with everyone working toward a common goal. This will involve standards and rules and changes that affect the taxpayers so that they realize that their contributions are making a huge difference.

Rafe Esquith is an elementary school teacher in Los Angeles who has written a book to chronicle his experiences in an inner city school. After reading of his work habits, I'm surprised he had the time. *There Are No Shortcuts* is an outstanding, insightful, educational, entertaining and inspirational book that will leave you smiling and infuriated at the same time. If all students, teachers, administrators and parents read this work, there would be very few problems today in our educational system.

My college years in the 1960s weren't the greatest time for me. This had to do with the fact that many of my teachers handed out too much work and at the same time were average or worse. You could say that they reached their level of incompetence and weren't really concerned about the students. In those days we dreaded two situations that were almost as bad as root canal surgery: open book tests and take home tests. An ordinary test requires study time and three hours in the classroom, but then it is over. With an open book test, the stress only increases and the instructor now feels he can make his test longer even if we are still only allowed three hours to reply.

Other disciplines may have had this same method of evaluation monitoring, so it wasn't limited to mathematics. As excruciating as being allowed to have a mathematics text open while being in a test situation, it got exponentially worse – after all, it was math – when we were handed a take home test. I don't have to tell you what I wanted to do with that test once my teacher gave it to me. If you got it on Friday, it meant you had the weekend to get it done. This didn't imply Friday, Saturday and Sunday but twenty-four hours each day, and that may not have been enough time. I recall one instance when I happened to come upon the answer to one of those questions in a math journal – I can't believe I actually had time to go through those boring publications. I copied the answer down as did my friend and we turned in the test. For that particular problem, we got two different grades and mine was the lower one.

Sister Mary Euthanasia: Johnny, your essay on "My Pet
     Fang" is the same as your brother's.
Johnny: Naturally, Sister. It's the same dog.

I asked my teacher why my credit for that question wasn't an A since the answer was right. It had to be since it was in the journal. He replied that he wasn't sure if I understood the problem. Beside grades being arbitrary, meaningless and final, we should have another adjective: bizarre.

I should get back to the "schule" in the title. You have heard of many people who have succeeded and never finished school. It wasn't pointed out that these persons didn't just drop out, they did something with their lives, mostly a lot of hard work. That's why they were successful. They weren't goof-offs and didn't settle for second best. It also wasn't mentioned that their leaving skool wasn't their choice. Many wanted to stay and get an education, but the depression had just hit and groceries were needed for the family. People living in other times faced and still face parallel situations. The majority of people who don't graduate will have a difficult time in the workplace. You shouldn't be able to leave where you are until you can spell it!

11

Sunday is a day of rest

In the first chapter, I indicated that we all need some rest and won't be able to function if breaks are not a part of our lives. Getting a break when it comes to getting a contract extended is one possible meaning of that word, and that's important, but here, I really mean a chance to recharge. I've have always felt that if you don't take a break, you'll have a breakdown. This is more applicable today with all the stress in corporat America. If that world doesn't clean up its act soon, all that will be left will be the cockroaches and *rats*.

Years ago, many stores were closed on Sunday. We had the blue laws, even in the red states. That has changed for a few reasons. Greed and competition enter into the equation but we shouldn't ignore the long workweek. Not long ago, I found a new no-frills supermarket – I had to buy my frills elsewhere, but I'm not sure which store carried them. This new store was only a small challenge for the big markets in western New York. It was open only on Monday through Saturday with shorter hours than the other food places. I was disappointed when I saw a sign on the store one day in 2006 that mentioned that soon they would be open on Sunday.

As far as I am concerned, if you can't buy your food without shopping on Sunday, you shouldn't be allowed to shop and will have to go a day without food. It's only twenty-four hours, so it's not that big an imposition. Before you disagree with me about my feelings in this regard, consider this: relying on that one day to get your groceries means that you are working too many hours or else your life is quite disorganized. The fifty or more hours a week is part of the problem, so I sympathize. Stopping to shop after work on a weekday will also solve the need to shop on the Sabbath. If you say that you're just too tired to do that, it only means that there's too much stress at the job or again, your day is too long. Installing a thirty-hour week will easily solve these problems.

Closing most businesses on Sunday will also mean that many workers won't need to put in time on that day – a great relief. Granted, there are some professions that don't have this option. You might argue that you like to go to dinner on that day, but many restaurants aren't open on that one day of the week anyway. Many companies will survive even if they are only open from Monday through Friday! Naturally, this will take some effort, but the cutback to thirty hours can play a huge part.

The sad part is that people aren't limited to work fifty or sixty hours a week. That has been "advanced" by the 24/7 society. Why should we restrict ourselves to a specific number of hours? You can be on call. I guess I shouldn't complain about having to work on Sunday when men and women today are saddled with being able to be called into work at any time. Salaried workers are never free to relax. Unfortunately, you could be a consultant in this same predicament. One of the contracts for which I interviewed gave me just that "opportunity." If I were on call, I am sure that the corporation wouldn't have paid me unless I actually showed up at the office. Since I really couldn't do very much had I been on call – like go to a movie, baseball game or a witchcraft convention at that time – I felt I should get paid for this waiting period. I feel the same about any salaried employee. Perhaps I didn't get the assignment because the interviewer sensed my attitude somehow while talking to me. It really was a pity because the place was three miles from my house – that would have been a nice commute.

Since I retired, I still work – I'm writing this book right now. The only difference is that I don't get paid. There are a few other things I do, so there is never a day when I'm bored. Buy a PC and you'll have more than enough work with all the crashes and incompetent software you run into every day. However, one day that I do almost nothing is Sunday. I read the paper and my efforts are limited to cooking, although in many cases I rely on food that was prepared the day before. *The Read My Lips Cookbook* was specifically intended to have you create delicious food without spending a great deal of time in the kitchen.

It wasn't that long ago that I didn't look forward to Sunday night. It was a time when I worked as a consultant in Rochester, New York. The trip was at least seventy miles from my house, so I had some long weeks – even if they were only four days! Do the calculation. I looked forward to Thursday afternoons since I had the next day off and the two after that. As great as that feeling was on those Thursdays, there was the complete opposite dread on Sunday nights. After all, I had to rise early to try to make it to the office at a reasonable hour. Getting there at nine meant that to put in a ten-hour day, I would have had to stay until seven p.m., something I wasn't about to do, especially on a Monday.

I also recall an instance some time ago when I was visiting friends in Georgia. We headed over to the university on that Sunday night. Seeing the lights in the library brought back too many memories of nights from college and grad school when I was spending time studying. I really would have preferred going out to dinner than be at that place. Fortunately, it wasn't long before we deserted the campus and headed over to their home.

One other effort of mine also made a huge difference in my work habits when I sold my house a few years ago. Houses are nice but you will have more work than if you rent an apartment or own a condominium. This is true even if you have a home that is maintenance free. Don't count on too many idle Sundays. Some say that working around the house or having a garden is very therapeutic. I can't argue with that but make sure your home doesn't get to be such a burden that you wind up spending each weekend working on the house, with very little rest. No matter how strapped you become, it can be worse: you could buy a "handyman's special." In that case, I hope you're better with tools than our plumber from a few chapters ago or the lumberjack I will mention later.

You might think that I miss my house, but I'm a lot happier in the condominium. There are fewer rooms to clean, I have no mortgage payments – I own it and no bank is entitled to even a part of it – and I don't shovel snow or cut grass anymore. The house did have a beautiful sunroom, which was great for every season of the year, but you make sacrifices for change and other benefits. I could have a skylight put into the place I live now, but the people above me would be furious. (That thought comes from the comedic genius of Steven Wright.)

You always hear people advising you to buy a house rather than live in an apartment. The reason is to have equity and something for your money. Why throw away your money renting? Whenever I rented a place, I always had something: a place to live, even if only temporarily. When you come down to it, it really depends on your situation, as sometimes it's better not to buy a home. There are disadvantages to each approach to living.

Buying means you get to write off the interest payment on the mortgage. This will help you on your taxes as you may get a refund rather have to make a payment. The more you spend for the home, the bigger the deduction, but you could default on the mortgage and lose the house. You won't have that problem if you are renting – well, you could get evicted for building a time machine in the basement. You can still get to deduct the interest if you buy a condominium. It's not quite the same as a house but you'll have less work.

I rented a place in New Hampshire in the early 1980s and after a couple years, had to move or else buy the unit as a condominium. I left and found a different apartment in Massachusetts, but maybe I should have done the conversion thing. I didn't take that option because I figured I would move out of the area shortly. Then again, not long after that, I bought condominiums in Brandon, Florida as well as in South Salem, New York. This was in the course of a year and I kept each for almost a decade but had tenants in each place after I moved out. I only lived in Florida for a few months and that investment may have been all right. However, I lived in the other condo in a town close to Connecticut between Richfield and New Canaan for almost three years, but I probably should have rented.

The reason I feel this way is because that place in New York cost me well over $150,000 – who would pay that much for a condo? I sold it a decade later for almost $50,000 less, while today you probably can't buy it for under $250,000. A few years before this I bought some land in the Poconos and had a log cabin built as a vacation home. We had a few great parties there, including a two-day Memorial Day celebration in 1983, but I probably shouldn't have gotten involved with that effort. If you are planning to make money in real estate, don't count on it.

As outrageous as the price of that condo was, before making my purchase, I looked at one that was selling for $230,000. I was even stupid enough to make an offer of $210,000 and thankfully, it wasn't enough for the sellers. Perhaps I wasn't so dumb as I came in with a low bid, but sometimes we have angels looking out for us! Had I bought that home, I'd probably still be making mortgage payments. It wasn't that long ago that I was in the Washington, DC area when I saw condos on sale for $300,000. Now, I'm sure you can't get them for that price, as the prices have been rising.

I should talk about the first house I bought. I was renting an apartment in Peekskill, New York, but I don't recall what I paid each month for rent. It probably was about the same as my first mortgage payment, but even so, I doubt that any bank would have given me a mortgage, even though I could have come up with the cash each month. The reason I got it was through the realtor, who verified that I would not default on the loan. Between the realtor, the bank and my dedication, I became what many people call an oxymoron, a *happy homeowner*.

The three-bedroom, two-story house cost about $50,000 in 1976 and through the years I had some major improvements done on it, some of which I did myself. I sold it in 1983 for about $80,000. Had I kept it for another year, I could have realized a quarter of a million dollars on the sale. I don't know what it would sell for today, maybe a hundred thousand dollars more than that. As far as my premature sale, it's only money and it can't buy happiness or good health. If you disagree with me on that point, you'll change your mind as you get to middle age.

What I still do not understand is this leap in the price of not only my first home but all the homes in Westchester County, where it was located. How does a residence increase by over two hundred percent in a single year? What amused me to no end were the people who didn't sell their homes and experienced this boost in home value, but then complained when the value of their $50,000 home dipped from $250,000 to $200,000. Greed will always be with us.

The saddest part of this situation is that these exorbitant prices mean that some people can't buy a home in that area. This is prevalent in such places as Boston, Los Angeles, Washington, DC, New York City and various other places across the land. If you grew up in an area, departed for college and returned, you may not have been able to buy a house or condo and live in your hometown. The price to rent may be too high as well. If home prices are through the roof, renting will be in line – they'll be unaffordable too. I find that very depressing and disheartening.

People still can get huge mortgages because today banks that wouldn't have honored my request years ago, will grant special balloon loans. These involve minimal payments initially but as time progresses, they skyrocket to the point that the mortgagee can't come up with the cash. The trapped homeowners' only option may be to sell, but even if that is successful, they might only be able to afford a tool shed in the same area. I hope it's insulated!

It's very difficult to relax if you have to live with outrageous mortgage payments. I bring that up because Sunday is a day of rest – at least that is what this chapter is all about. Too many people are workaholics for some reason, but along the way, they have no idea how to relax. I once dated a woman who said she had to keep busy. You also hear people say, "He's so busy," "I didn't do anything today," or "I've got to run." If you didn't do anything, you can't get arrested. Why do people have any guilt about not doing anything? Didn't they get out of bed? I think that's something – you'll really agree with me on that if you have surgery. What is the last individual running from? It sounds like she's trying to get away from doing nothing, which is not a bad thing.

Actress Gwyneth Paltrow recently got into a pinch after making a few comments in a press conference that she conducted in Spanish in December 2006. My friend Gary told me of her quote which I thought was quite pertinent to this book. Part of what she said was, "The British are much more intelligent and civilized than the Americans," but she didn't allow for the fact that a person with the brain of a kohlrabi doesn't allow for differences in languages. Personally, I think she had a good point, even with the way it was translated and some people just can't handle the truth.

She apologized and added, "I said that Europe is a much older culture and there's a difference. I always say *in America, people live to work and in Europe, people work to live.* There are positives in both." She added: "Obviously I need to go back to seventh grade Spanish." Brad, I think you made a mistake.

12

Work *can* kill you

I'm sure you've heard the expression, "Work won't kill you," more times that you can recall or want to hear. Well, it's a huge myth. Too many people have died and continue to do so in the coal mines, from gas explosions and on various other jobs. You may have heard about Bhopal and the tragic accident there on December 2, 1984. You can read about it in *Five Past Midnight in Bhopal* by Dominique Lapierre and Javier Moro, but I hope you have a strong stomach. What about all the victims who gave their lives and are dying even as I write this from the accident in Chernobyl that took place on April 25, 1986, which Alla Yaroshinskaya describes in *Chernobyl: the Forbidden Truth.* Both books are excellent reads for the day before a colonoscopy.

I'm all in favor of technology – to a point – but too many people have perished in attempts at space exploration, work at chemical plants and building the bomb. Howard Hughes barely survived a plane crash and had he succumbed, it's possible that aviation wouldn't be what it is today. His injuries took place because although adventurous and daring, he may have felt he was invincible. You can read about him in *The Untold Story of Howard Hughes* by Peter Harry Brown and Pat H. Broeske. Progress is fraught with sacrifice; many have died building bridges, tunnels, and skyscrapers.

You may have thought that working at a computer terminal in an office is without risk, but tell that to those who never left the World Trade Center on September 11, 2001. I'm not so sure that the CRT and PC may not be causes of cancer as I spent time in front of those devices for over a quarter of a century as a consultant and went through cancer surgery more than once. That's another story.

I was a teacher for eight years and that seemed to be a safe choice, but Columbine changed all that. If your assignment is in the inner city schools, your stress levels could easily rise. Before I was to start an assignment teaching part-time in the Binghamton School System in the Southern Tier of New York State, I had some apprehension. After all, it was a city school. However, the students were so laid back that I asked some of the kids who their supplier was. This was not your typical city school, though.

There are a few jobs that I didn't have or wouldn't do. From the jobs that I landed over the years, there was no job I refused unless it was unethical or dangerous. I wanted to have a chance at other jobs. This does not say that I didn't work for corporations that did shady things – I just didn't realize it at the time. I worked at an ornamental iron shop in Buffalo, and I'm happy to report that today, I have all my fingers. I had a contract at a nuclear power plant in Oswego, New York, but I left as soon as I could, after hearing about Chernobyl and Three Mile Island. On other occasions, it wasn't until after I got into the assignment that I realized that the corporation was probably a subsidiary of Tyco or WorldCom. Once I had the knowledge, it didn't take me long to depart, no matter what it paid.

Dangerous work, such as being a spy, assassin, consultant on duty in Iraq, soldier or policeman is not without high financial rewards, but you probably won't have to worry about your retirement years, which could be very short or non-existent. Being an officer of the law may be the only one of these jobs that is ethical. Unfortunately, our tax dollars pay for many of these dangerous occupations. If you'd like to really get infuriated about where your money goes, read ***Blowing My Cover: My Life as a CIA Spy*** by Lindsay Moran. I won't reveal the ending but should emphasize that it's non-fiction, which you won't put down until you finish reading.

Working at a post office at one time was free of danger, but from some events involving gunplay, *going postal* has taken on a completely different meaning, and it's not pretty. I don't advocate shooting Newman but that may not have been such a bad idea. However, then we would have been deprived of a few good laughs on Seinfeld. Having a delivery route in the country is certainly good for your health until a hurricane, twister or earthquake greeting arrives to spice up your day. It's not any better when you're pitted against the Dobermans and bull-like dogs on your route.

I took a short vacation to Acadia National Park in Maine after Labor Day in 2006, visiting nearby Little Cranberry Island. When I was there, it was absolutely beautiful, but unfortunately the weather that I experienced that week was not the norm. The people live there year round and have to make a living off the water, doing it as lobster gatherers. Some do it the entire year. That can't be much fun in December and January. This profession is not limited to one sex. You can read about a young woman's ocean adventures in any of the books of Linda Greenlaw. *The Lobster Chronicles* relates her experience in the Atlantic and I especially liked *All Fishermen Are Liars*.

Others who catch crab, cod and tuna don't have it easy either, despite the remunerations. At times the catch might be a bit less than expected and this affects what winds up in the fisherman's wallet. You may have seen or read *The Perfect Storm* – the story chronicling one group that didn't return from their fishing adventure. This is one disaster that repeats year after year. With great adventure and good pay also comes inevitable risk.

Journalists are another class of people who put their lives in great jeopardy, especially when they are assigned to cover war, which seems to be never-ending. As you probably know, for most of them the pay is nowhere near the danger involved. During the World Wars there was the belief that getting to the theatre of war was romantic and the place to be. It's a wonder that this idea wasn't included in a Disney episode in Fantasyland.

A job with the National Guard in order to get an education seemed like a great opportunity. In many cases, it was the only way for some to escape their crime-infested neighborhood. That changed drastically when they received orders to Vietnam or Iraq. Not that many people are really into quagmires! This deployment resulted even after the recruit was assured that seeing action on the front lines would never happen. Of course, things only got worse when the "tour" – that word doesn't seem to fit – of duty was complete but there was a call to return to Iraq for a bonus year or two. No one should have to be a soldier.

There will always be conflagrations so we will always need firemen. These men and women serve us by putting their lives at risk with every call at the firehouse, except the one to get the keg refilled. I will have a few more words on these brave individuals who gave of themselves in the hours after the tragedy on 9/11.

Another duty I wouldn't care to have is that of a White House secret service policeman. Let me see if I understand this: I have to get in the way so that the bullet doesn't reach the president. Does that come with benefits? I probably won't need to worry about paying my MasterCard bill. The job of a bodyguard can't be easy, but it does pay quite well, as does being born into a mob family. In the case of the latter, the work is never boring, the hours are irregular and you meet all kinds of people, some of whom you may even want to know as friends and have over for parties – check all guns at the door. When you go out to dinner, you may want to sit with your back to the wall.

Speaking of food, another occupation that you may have thought was relatively safe was the restaurant business. You may not have heard of the goings on in Umberto's in New York City. There are three names for the red stuff in Italian restaurants: sauce, gravy and blood. In addition, the Seinfeld episode when Elaine purportedly had a big head illustrates that even a fork can be used to require a bit of surgery for someone who is a bad breaker-upper. Waiting on tables might be all right, but things change for the worse when you go behind the kitchen doors. Bill

Buford wrote a book about his journey as a butcher in Italy and his apprenticeship as a cook in the kitchen of Multo Mario in New York. *Heat: an Amateur's Adventures as Kitchen Slave, Line Cook, Pasta Maker, and Apprentice to a Dante-quoting Butcher in Tuscany* is educational, entertaining and points out that being a line cook could be a way to get into the emergency room in short order. It also has a never-ending title, but that is not why I read it.

I need to return to a group of people I discussed earlier whose lives were greatly affected by work: slaves. If you've never picked cotton, let me assure you that it is backbreaking, the sun is intolerable and dishpan hands would be welcome compared to the appendages of those of the slaves in the field. A job can't be that good if someone would drown himself in preference to returning to face his master.

Even though it's fiction, *The Jungle* by Upton Sinclair, points out the abominable conditions in the meatpacking industry of a hundred years ago. We can see conditions just as bad today in the plants across the country that give us wings, steaks, pork chops, ribs and bacon. If someone gets hurt on the job, there's a good chance that when she returns, her job will have been filled by someone else. Chances are the company won't pay the hospital bills, either.

Too many industries have safety regulations but somehow they aren't observed. If the Occupational Safety and Health Administration (OSHA) is short-staffed, it will really be difficult to police the industry. This will result in unreported violations and what's much worse, injury to the employees. I recall more than one occasion during my supermarket days when the box cutter found a different target than was intended and I was driven to a nearby hospital for stitches. I wasn't the only one who got scars from the job.

These types of accidents can't be completely avoided, but when management demands more of the workers than is physically possible, this creates a feeling of weariness in the help, which only results in still more injuries. A minimum wage or less and few benefits, if any, doesn't make the situation any better for these men and women at the plant.

If things weren't dangerous enough, another kind of problem arises. This has to do with the effects of the business. I mentioned bomb building earlier, but you can get a better idea of how unsafe the entire process was from the book, *Making a Real Killing* by Len Ackland. It details what really was involved in the process throughout the country at the Hanford Reservation in the state of Washington, Oak Ridge in Tennessee, Ellenton, South Carolina, the home of the Savannah River plant and Los Alamos, New Mexico. There is special emphasis on Rocky Flats, just outside Denver, which in 1995, the U. S. Department of Energy labeled the most dangerous weapons plant in the nation because of the health and safety risks.

There are a few other industries that may pay well, but you may want to avoid. There is an area in Texas and Louisiana called Cancer Alley. It is dominated by big business and the chemical companies, who developed polyvinyl chloride, or PVC, a type of plastic. Vinyl chloride is a colorless flammable gas that goes into making PVC. Today, you can see PVC or vinyl everywhere in all kinds of products.

Mossville is a predominately African-American town near Lake Charles, Louisiana with four polyvinyl chloride facilities. Production began in the middle of the twentieth century when various companies began producing plastic. Many of them found that this endeavor was hazardous to the health of the employees. The federal Agency for Toxic Substances has shown that breathing vinyl chloride for long periods of time can result in damage to the liver and nerves and cause liver cancer and immune reactions. The corporations had knowledge of these dangers but failed to inform the workers of them. Instead they developed a plan to cover up this problem and PVC saw no decrease in output.

But the health of the laborers was affected. The chemicals involved were so devastating that some of the bones in the hands of those in the plant actually dissolved. Others suffered brain damage from being on the scene and there were other problems as well. Eventually, these companies were exposed, but not before too many workers had perished or suffered severe consequences. I need not tell you that the air, land and water nearby were also devastated.

In Venice, Italy, PVC was produced as well, and workers suffered from many illnesses and died. The widows of the deceased had a lawsuit, but not against the corporation producing vinyl. Rather, the defendants in the case were executives of the company, and the charge was manslaughter. Unfortunately, justice was not served as the plaintiffs lost in their efforts. While this was occurring, this foreign company conspired with its sister companies in the United States to guarantee that PVC was judged by the American people to be a safe product, despite all that had happened indicating exactly the opposite.

A job that can't be good for anyone's health is spraying chemicals on lawns, fruits and vegetables. The process of using toxic weed or pest killers is a huge danger to the applicator. I grew honeydew melons, tomatoes, red cabbage, okra, Swiss chard, peaches and other produce in my garden, but I refused to spray any chemical on the crop. Instead, I let nature take its course and a bug or two was no big deal. I'd rather not have a worm stare at me from the apple I am eating, but after all, it is protein and the alternative is poison, which doesn't add much flavor to the produce.

The gunk that is applied to lawns may keep out the weeds, but besides the danger to the sprayer, the process will poison the land, air and people close-by. The company posts those signs that warn you to stay away from the grass for a couple days. What makes you think that it will be safe for pets and humans after forty-eight hours? Remember that the poison has to wind up somewhere. That is another job that I don't recommend.

Besides working for Chem-lawn or at the vinyl plant, there probably aren't many safe jobs at any chemical companies. *Better living through chemistry* didn't quite achieve all it set out to do. I actually liked chemistry in school and even thought about pursuing a career in that subject, but I decided on mathematics, instead. It's a lot safer discipline and you won't blow yourself up.

Working at a landfill can't be any picnic, even if you have no olfactory capability. Actually, the hydrogen sulfide produced at these dumps can destroy your sense of smell. What you can't experience with your nose may be worse than what you can. Because of all the misdeeds of various corporations, like Hooker Chemical, Exxon, Kodak and General Electric, quite a few high paying jobs resulted. Someone has to clean up the mess, but once again the danger involved can't be underestimated. These are jobs that shouldn't have been necessary in the first place and I firmly believe that those who are responsible for the polluting should do the cleanup, besides being fined. Maybe there is a reason why prisons are still being built.

If you get on the highway, you'll see another risky job. Someone has to collect the tolls on the interstate. Walking along a highway isn't that good for anyone's system but how would you like to be stationed for eight hours in the middle of the Holland Tunnel? If the claustrophobia doesn't get you, then the fumes will. There has got to be a better way to make a buck, no matter what it involves.

It's not easy being an officer of the law. Those who roam the highways to uphold the law and apprehend speeders on the road have quite a challenge. There aren't too many spouses, parents or siblings who aren't concerned for the well-being of their beloved, fearing they may never return. A bulletproof vest won't stop bullets fired at someone's head and with continuing advances in weaponry, each passing day becomes ever more dangerous.

The highways seem to always be under construction and this provides plenty of work but also more danger. With the lunacy of some drivers, it's probably not even safe to be on break as you could be a casualty there just as well. Two requisites for working on road construction, whether you hold a stop / slow sign or do the grading, is good eyesight – so you can see them coming at you – and being able to move fast so you won't get run down. I already mentioned breathing the toxic emissions as another threat.

A few months ago a friend sent me an email with a panoramic picture of the Highest Bridge in the World. It was scheduled to be completed in January 2005 and I assume that the project is done. I'm not thrilled at looking down from the top of a skyscraper or a high point on a cliff – that's an understatement. The Millau Viaduct Project is in southern France and it is up in the sky – it has the highest bridge piers in world and the tallest is 240 meters high. Overall height is an outstanding 336.4 meters. I'm sorry I didn't convert these dimensions to feet for you. For more details, check out http://bridgepros.com/projects/Millau_Viaduct/

The bridge was engineered so that people don't have to drive on all those mountain roads, which are scary and dangerous. I'm not sure this creation is any better. I certainly won't drive on it, even if I were wearing brown pants. I can't imagine building this replacement for all the highways that were down below. This thirty-nine month construction project was financed privately. Perhaps it is one idea whose time should never have come – it might be better than the bridge in Alaska to nowhere, though.

Granted, there have been great engineering feats over the years to make our lives better, but was it really worth the risk for the laborers? You may not have been bothered by the fatalities that have occurred on these endeavors, but you would have felt much different if you had lost a loved one because of one of these projects. Unfortunately, there are workers today involved in the coal, oil, nuclear and gas industry who face the same challenges each day that those who worked on that bridge in France.

A very intriguing proposal comes from a group of labor unions led by the Steelworkers, Machinists and Electrical Workers. The Apollo Project calls for investing $300 billion over a ten-year period to create new energy based on efficiency and innovation. This would involve energy-efficient buildings and appliances, environmentally friendly factories, hybrid vehicles and mass transit. The program would create three million manufacturing jobs and the cost for the entire project would be only a fraction of what the country spends each year on imported oil.

I'm not sure that we should throw away vast sums of money on any mission to Mars. Maybe if we could send lawyers, politicians, agents and businessmen, then I may not object – as long as it happened to be a one-way trip. Why not invest in what is here on earth? Heaven knows there's plenty that can be done to make life better for the poor, homeless, unemployed and suffering.

The people who gave of their time in the hours after the collapse of the World Trade Center suffered with asthma, cancer and other problems because of the toxicity of the area, with some giving their lives. This happened because officials said that the site was safe, but time has shown that to not be the case. After all, what came tumbling down was what was left of personal computers and other electronic equipment, asbestos and chemicals found in buildings, and don't forget about the jet fuel. It doesn't take much thought to realize that even with body protection, ground zero was dangerously contaminated and would be for some time. I was in New York in October 2001, but wanted no part of visiting the World Trade Center site.

Even if an office is free from toxic substances – I can't figure out how that could be achieved today – there is another danger, which I have already alluded to in an earlier chapter. This is the health problem created from long hours, such as stress-induced heart attacks, high blood pressure, stomach ailments and the side effects of addictions, such as excessive alcohol abuse. Too many professions expect their employees to put in outrageous hours. Being a lawyer or accountant is no picnic, especially in the latter's days before April 15 each year.

Not long ago I was to join a friend and his girlfriend for dinner, but the latter couldn't make it – she was too busy with her job. She had quit it but then went back to her boss on condition that her hours would be limited. You can guess how long that agreement lasted. She is still working long hours at that job. The last I heard, these two were no longer a couple. Jobs can be dangerous but they can also be habit-forming – neither of which is good for anyone. This might suggest that one of the best things to overcome this problem is an early retirement. It is up to each of us to get to the point where we will actually be able to pull that off.

13
Thresholds

I can't emphasize enough that stress can kill you, whether you get it from working or from some other source. In November 2005, I traveled south to Savannah, Daytona Beach and Charleston for a short vacation as well as the warmer weather. My second stop was in Raleigh, North Carolina to visit my friends Thomas and Linda, whom I had not seen in a few years. I got directions from a combination of Yahoo Maps, MapQuest – I think it should more appropriately be called Mapguess – and Streets and Maps, a Microsoft product that I bought. The reason I didn't settle on one single map design software was because of the notoriety of all of these. You just can't trust them.

Following the directions, I arrived in the general Raleigh area about 3:30 in the afternoon. That's the good news. The bad news is that I made it to my friends' house at 6:30, three hours later. I blame myself somewhat, because I should have gotten an actual map or at least more specific layout of the streets where my friends resided, since I hadn't been there before. They had recently moved. The main fault was in the incorrect directions provided. I can't emphasize enough to make sure you know where you're going. In the process of getting lost, at 4 o'clock, I was okay. By 6 p.m., I had surpassed my threshold of tolerance. I was stressed out because someone didn't do his job when they produced these directions.

Too many times these instructions are off the mark. You'll be told to turn left when you really ought to go right – maybe they figure your last name is Columbus. At other times you are told to go straight ahead but that's hard to do when you come to a T in the road – not the kind you wear – and you can only go right or left. On my trip to Maine, I had decent directions until I wanted to get from Bar Harbor to Hooksett, New Hampshire. I was on Mt. Desert Island and I figured the route back would be similar to the way I came, except for the last part. In all, I guessed that this would be about 250 miles or so. The route mapped out using Streets and Maps was by way of Nova Scotia. I really want to get to that part of Canada someday, but not on this venture. Perhaps the software realized that I had been driving quite a bit and that's why they put me on the ferry – I could get a bit of rest.

I'm not sure which map software you should trust. From my experience, you should probably get three sets of directions and then survey them to determine how to get to where you are going. Of course, then you would be spending so much time finding the right route that you may not feel like going anywhere – another example of unnecessary work. I find it particularly amusing to see these exact words on the MapQuest disclosure statement:

These directions are informational only. No representation is made or warranty given as to their content, road conditions or route usability or expeditiousness. User assumes all risk of use. MapQuest and its suppliers assume no responsibility for any loss or delay resulting from such use.

If I am not mistaken, one of these driving direction tools even advises users to take a test run of the route to their destination. Let me get this straight: I am planning a late December trip to Myrtle Beach. I need to go through a practice session before I actually make the journey in earnest. With gas costing three bucks a gallon, that's a great idea! No further questions, your honor.

Returning to my thoughts on thresholds, I had one software contract in Rochester in the early 1990s when we were doing some major changes to the existing system. The programming changes were made so we had to get on with the system testing, which was scheduled for an entire week. This is a normal procedure and it was set up to have some of the people – this included the consultants – be at work from eight in the morning until whatever time management dismissed them. The second shift, of which I was a part, came in and stayed until the leaders were satisfied. As you can imagine, these sessions dragged on and there were times when I wanted to suggest that we all go home, get some rest and return refreshed the next day. This was the reasonable thing to do, but I'm not a manager so it wasn't done and I didn't even bother to offer this idea, since it would have fallen on deaf ears.

This scenario demonstrates why we hated being there as the threshold had been reached. This was the case during the 1960s when I was filled with days of college studies as well as supermarket bliss. Each of these situations is burnout on a short-term basis, even though my undergraduate days and post graduate work in that decade covered only six years. Of course, other factors can enter into the picture, such as control, incompetence and boring work, as I have already mentioned.

There is a definite correlation between thresholds and burnout. Someone could work at a job for forty hours a week for ten years and get burned out while someone who opened up a restaurant, slaved sixty hours each week for twenty years may not be suffering from the same effect. Notice that I used the words "may not." Even so, quite a few factors enter into burnout, some of which I have touched on earlier.

I experienced another type of threshold that needs to be discussed since it is quite common in the workplace. I loved math in school, but I had one concern. After the lesson, I was comfortable with what I had been taught, but I feared the next day I wouldn't comprehend the subject matter. That would change things dramatically. You could call this a comfort threshold and I reached it sometime in college mathematics courses. My classmates and I called this phenomenon "getting snowed," and it had nothing to do with the fact that Canisius College and the university I attended immediately afterwards are in Buffalo. This happens in Southern California and Florida just as well.

As you can tell, this is another reason why we have difficulty in the workplace. I obtained a degree in computer science and when I started my first job in the business world, I was fairly comfortable with computer programming. Leaving to become a consultant tended to diminish this comfort level. With every new contract – and I certainly had a few – the first day was always the hardest for this reason. There were two considerations to bring on these feelings of insecurity. First, I had to deal with how the company worked, and this is what everyone goes through with a new job. That may be why people are reluctant to change jobs. The second factor is the computer system and all that can be involved.

Fortunately, the latter difficulty was no big deal since I was working with computers – it was my job. You hear so many people say that they don't have nor want a PC. The newness or change from the norm is one problem but perhaps they don't want to be involved with the crashes and bugs that are so common, no matter what type of monster they have. I taught high school math for eight years and always felt comfortable in front of the class, except when my principal came in to observe me. After all, I was human.

I didn't quite feel the same way when I was in front of a class with anything to do with computers. I taught COBOL courses, but I had spent years actually programming in that language, which is the COmmon Business Oriented Language used in corporat America – some of those in charge there could care a rat's *you know what* about the people. As I mentioned earlier, COBOL was supposed to be replaced years ago, but on the last contract I had in 2001, it was still around. Of course, I would still rather teach math than computers any day. The problem with the computer world is that there are so many software packages and systems and so much to learn. This demands specialization, but even the people who are supposed to be experts can't answer many of the routine questions asked them. I've experienced this on too many occasions when I've called the help desk.

COBOL is a language that I worked with for close to a quarter of a century. I managed to program that language on IBM mainframes, DEC systems and Wang computers as well as on networked PCs. Even after all that involvement, there were times when I learned something new about the language. It was complicated, but I found it was well designed and with great possibilities. However, the software we see today doesn't come close to it with all the bugs and design flaws. You can see why very few people are comfortable in these *disciplines* – probably that's an inappropriate word here – and that includes the nerds. This is precisely why the arrival of technology is another huge factor in why we hate work.

As I already mentioned, when I was a consultant, on most occasions, I had two bosses: one from the company as well as the representative from the consulting firm. You could get stuff thrown at you from different directions and the same thing happens with technology, whose environment and all its headaches reduces your threshold for pain and increases your hate. At the same time, computers give us the opportunity to put in longer hours, when we just want to go home. Before, a task took four hours and now, thanks to technology, it takes six. The number of reasons why we hate work seems to be almost endless.

14
Women priests

When you write, you are limited to what you can say. In my manual for workaholics, I didn't talk at all about the labor-obsessed and possessed in the clergy. These include priests, nuns, brothers, rabbis and a few others, but not necessarily the neo-conservatives. Ministering people work long hours just like the rest of us for many of the same reasons. If God intended us to work such long hours, we would have been born with union cards. This chapter will deal with that problem of the religious life and I will not limit it to one sex – hence the title.

I never entered the seminary but know a few priests, including my brother Nicholas, who is a Conventual Franciscan. In a few years he will have been in the order for a half century – he entered young! From time to time I ask priests to come over for dinner or to get together for some reason. On all too many occasions, they can't make it – they're too busy. I dropped off some books at the Franciscan Center and asked if Father Joe was around. He wasn't but that didn't surprise me. On most of my visits there, he isn't on the premises. Maybe it's time for me to stop doing pop-ins! Nevertheless, you could say he works too much and he's not the only one. Many individuals never realized when they joined an order that their days would be so filled with work.

One reason for the long hours could be the shortage of priests. We also have seen the closing of many churches in the cities and the subsequent rise of the large parishes in the suburbs. Faiths other than Roman Catholic have seen huge growth in their populations, including mammoth churches and Hollywood productions at the services – not my idea of what Christ would want, despite Mel Gibson. At the same time, if there are so many religious people, why is there so much social injustice in the world today?

I won't bore you with scandals in churches, no matter what denomination. You can read – *In God's Name: an Investigation into the Murder of John Paul I* by David A. Yallop, *The Popes against the Jews: the Vatican's Role in the Rise of Modern anti-Semitism* by David I. Kertzer and *The Making of the Pope 2005* by Andrew M. Greeley for some insight, not all bad. Some deplorable behavior has led to the noted deficiencies in the work force, but you can't blame it all on that. The question is what to do about it. One solution is obvious from the title of this chapter. Another option is the possibility of married priests. When you really think about it, many in the religious life commit to poverty, chastity and obedience. Since all these men and women are human when they profess these vows and remain so afterwards, these promises might be a bit too much. *Two out of three ain't bad* – as Meatloaf sang in his smash hit – may be a better idea. Either or both ideas of married priests and female ministers – each found in many religions today – would reduce the shortage of needed clergy.

Many will contend that the church – it could be any that doesn't have married leaders – can't afford it financially. After all, who is going to pay for the shopping sprees of the priests' wives and husbands at Macy's? Then there is the cost of retirement and benefits to the spouse after a priest's passing. But, it is very possible that had the church allowed wedded people into the rectory, much of the pedophilia scandal may not have occurred, saving oodles of dough. These funds could have been used to solve that money problem although there probably needs to be a limit on the number of pairs of shoes that the missus can purchase.

I have never visited there, but there also seems to be a great deal of cash in Rome. I'm not suggesting the closing down of Vatican City and having a moving garage sale, but this preoccupation with the affordability of coupling might be a bit overblown. You could argue that I am not qualified to offer suggestions on church matters since I am not part of the clergy and I don't live in the Vatican, but over the years, priests and sisters have advised the married! Indeed, I am part of the church since the people – even the lay members – all participate. We are the ones who make it up.

People tell me – priests mostly – that priests can't or shouldn't be married, but a few years ago that possibility existed. You can read a wonderful chronicle in *Vows: the Story of a Priest, a Nun and Their Son* by Peter Manseau, whom I met recently. If you haven't figured it out, he is relating the story of his parents as well as his own. His parents weren't rebels, but his father felt that change was coming in the church and consequently married a former nun.

If priests can't be married, didn't the apostles have wives? (I won't accept the argument that Judas wasn't married – he had a tough time getting dates, let alone any kind of commitment. Who can blame any woman? They heard about him.) For you religious scholars reading this, I'm kidding about that apostle, but not about the others. Some time ago, a friend of mine was ordained a priest and he met a woman. That is not unusual – clergy are allowed to talk to the opposite sex – except that he fell in love with her. He decided to alter his life and left the church and married her, since the Catholic Church wouldn't allow him to tie the knot. Many say you can't have two masters – an argument that I don't accept for not having married priests. Anyone who enters into matrimony has at least two masters! My friend eventually became a minister in the Presbyterian Church, so he is still a preacher of the faith.

Married priests have been around for some time. Celibacy wasn't introduced in the first century, so spouses were in the rectory – or wherever they resided – for many years. Since the times change, the church must do so as well, although these ideas need not be drastic and radical. I don't read many novels but one Sunday at Mass, Father Robert Wood recommended a book by

Morris West, *The Clowns of God*. I must have liked the book and especially the writer – that usually follows – since I have read over twenty of his books, all fiction. West is very insightful and progressive in his thinking, even if I found it in his novels. I can only recommend that other religious people – clergy and lay men and women alike – see what he has to offer in his writing.

I mentioned that clergy advise married couples, so allowing the former to get married would certainly give them more insight into that sacrament. If this change doesn't happen, what will probably take place is such a shortage that eventually those in the sacristy and sanctuary will be the lay people, deacons and sisters, replacing those with the collars. Of course, this is what the church really is – all of us serving others. However, why not allow priests to marry today, thus eliminating this crisis in the future?

I mentioned retirement in the church and many can't do so because they have no pension. I doubt that the diocese pays into social security so priests and nuns can't file at sixty-five. However, in their old age they are taken care of by the order, which in turn is supported by donations from the parishioners. There is a tradeoff as retirement age gets delayed to the point that clergy in their sixties still work, even if their hours are reduced somewhat. So if they worked sixty hours a week before, does that mean that their workload will now be only forty hours? That is not my idea of retirement.

As far as women priests goes, if my brother agrees that priests should be married, maybe I'll not push the issue of females saying Mass. Naturally, that will upset many women. Of course, there are ministers of that gender in many churches – I met one at a "stop the war" demonstration in September 2006 and she offered eloquent and inspiring thoughts. We have nuns and mother superiors and even sisters who think they run the parish – I'll write anything for a laugh. Why not allow women priests? They make up over half the church and weren't they the majority of the spectators at Calvary when Christ was hanging on the cross? The disciples went AWOL and they weren't even in the National Guard.

All throughout history, women have been denigrated as second-class citizens. In the past the nuns did much of the instruction of the children in the schools. I don't recall any teachers that didn't look like penguins in my parochial school days. Women take care of the sanctuary of the church all year long and are hard pressed during Christmas and Easter seasons. They also cook the meals for the pastor and clean the rectory. If we don't allow women priests, at least acknowledge the fact that the female population played an important role in the church throughout the ages.

The clergy are people just like the doctors, nurses, consultants, coal miners and mob bosses. Each can be overworked but nuns and priests have further difficulties. The obvious shortage and low remuneration enter into the equation, despite the fact that their room and board is usually taken care of. They are still human beings and remedies for them having better lives are no different than for the people in the pews.

15
Health care

Doctors and nurses are another great example of workaholics, some by choice. This occupation works people to death and not only do those in the profession suffer health problems, on too many occasions their patients don't make out too well either. You've probably heard of individuals who had the wrong leg amputated or the patient whose gall bladder was taken when he came in for a colonoscopy. The latter gave up something two days in a row when that wasn't prescribed. Without great health care, a society can only wither and die.

My cousin is a health care provider and she gets off from work for four days in succession. The bad news is that she puts in twelve-hour shifts for three days in a row. As you can see, this is a few more hours than the goal of the thirty-hour workweek. She is not alone as many nurses and doctors are trapped in fifty-hour weeks and more. This is due to the shortage in the field. Some love what they are doing so much that they can't take themselves away from the job. They are to be applauded, but it would be more beneficial to hire more help and give these people raises while reducing their hours. In their zeal, these doctors and nurses may have involuntarily become workaholics.

As with any occupation, there are those who put in the long hours for many reasons, one of which is greed. This is not good for them or the patients, as I have already stated. Just as a consultant can't be that productive in an environment where she is asked to be on the job for fifty hours a week, the same applies to those in the health care field. Don't believe a doctor who tells you otherwise. By now you should realize that doctors don't know everything! I also think that because of the high stress levels in hospitals, even a forty-hour workweek is too much.

You won't be able to get assistance and relief for the help if there are no people to fill the positions. To entice more people to the field, there is not much need to raise the salaries of the doctors, since they seem to be doing fine in that regard, but don't overlook the fact that they do have high insurance costs. Reducing their workload should result in their being more effective, resulting in fewer lawsuits. Raising the pay of the nurses as well as limiting their hours should make a big difference, with more recruits.

There are a few other things that need to be done as well. The first has to do with revamping health insurance. With skyrocketing costs and mismanagement, you may just as well have no plan. Something needs to be done to limit these expenses. I present what has to be done without the actual solution. All I know is that what we have now does not help those people who need health care; the employees are overworked and stressed out and there is too much waste and fraud in the system. Changes need to be made.

The people in the system have to pitch in too. For example, some with health insurance will visit the doctor at the first sign of a cold or when they break a bone. Well, maybe the fractures need to be checked out, but too many patients feel that since they have coverage, they should use it. This attitude only indicates that someone else who needs assistance may be waiting longer for care with a more serious concern. There is also the strain placed on health care people, as if their days weren't long enough already.

The one suffering needs to have some knowledge of medicine and the human body so as to limit visits. After my first cancer, I wanted nothing to do with researching the causes. After the passage of time, I got more involved and this reaction is only to be expected. Nonetheless, each of us has to be more responsible about his own health, as well as that of her beloved. This means that we should probably not visit McDonalds every day for dinner. Instead see the movie, *Super Size Me* and read the companion book, ***Fast Food Nation: the Dark Side of the all-American Meal*** by Eric Schlosser. You'll never eat at a fast food restaurant again. The book was also made into a non-documentary movie of the same name.

I'm not telling you to change your diet to soy burgers and rice cakes. In fact, you may want to limit your soy intake since it may not be that great a substitute for anything. As far as rice cakes go, if you haven't figured out that they don't taste much better than Styrofoam – which you should avoid – this warning should save you the expense of trying them. I'll never be a vegan, but I have leaned more towards the practice of vegetarianism, which is not a cult and you don't have to contact my family since I haven't been abducted as I write this. I still eat meat, but not as much as I used to.

Moderation is the secret to enjoying food as opposed to having to get an angioplasty after sitting down to a thirty-two ounce steak. This small change in diet should limit your doctor visits to checkups rather than trips to the emergency room. After my encounters – if you haven't already figured it out – I really don't care to have surgery of any kind, if it can be avoided. That should be your goal too, and it will benefit the doctors and nurses as well as people in hospital beds or those waiting for one.

Another aspect of medicine that my system isn't too thrilled about is taking antibiotics and drugs. While recovering after surgery, I had the pleasure of trying a few drugs to reduce some of the pain as well as to prevent other problems that may have resulted. Demerol and Darvoset may offer relief after surgery, but they are not without other difficulties. I can vouch for that because the pill I took at home may have seemed to help provide some relief, but at the same time I had the worst case of constipation in my life. It wasn't worth taking the painkiller to get that result. This seems to be true about most drugs. Even if it appears that some pill really works without side effects, it is very possible that somewhere down the road the user will have to pay. This is besides the premiums.

I was introduced to Tequin, Levaquin and Cipro in the year 2004. You will notice that the first letter of each represents TLC – I really hate acronyms. In each case when I took the tablet, I didn't get constipated, but just the opposite. It wasn't a fun time. Maybe I should have taken some Darvoset at the same time and hoped for a standoff, something I would have preferred – in my case standing would have been a blessing! After my adventures, I heard that Cipro – the mother of all antibiotics, appropriately enough – was used against anthrax. Those are three nasty pills that I hope to never, ever see again.

In the summer of 2006, I had a minor case of gout. I visited my doctor but didn't see him. Instead his assistant prescribed an antibiotic, cephalexin – not to be used unless necessary – and two anti-inflammatories, colchicine and indomethacin. The documentation accompanying the pills wasn't very assuring. One recommended contacting my local poison center in case of an overdose while another warned of the risk of serious and sometimes fatal heart problems. I didn't feel like taking any of this stuff, despite my big toe troubles, but did wind up taking the absolute minimum of each anti-inflammatory after four meals. I am not convinced that any of these drugs had any effect since my pain seemed to be disappearing by the time I started ingesting the tablets.

Drugs or surgery may be needed at times, but too many doctors never consider alternatives. They seem to be nothing more than *cut and run* people – they do surgery and run to the next patient. They also make you run to the pharmacist. Our society is so tuned in to the television culture of drug advertising that we are out of touch with our own bodies. The knowledge of all the possible side effects should get us to make some changes in our lives and use drugs only as a very last resort. Even if some chemical can prevent some initial suffering, remember that getting through it without the pill may result in a great deal less pain later. Too many side effects from drugs just aren't worth it.

As I've said, working too many hours causes stress and many health problems, which in turn generate problems for doctors and nurses since they have to work longer hours. Even if we are not overcome in any way from the long days at the office, the situation may lead us to unhealthy eating habits – such as stopping in at Burger King – which then can get you to the medicine cabinet for some drug that you shouldn't have needed in the first place. I used to love the Whopper, but you won't catch me in any of those places again.

I hope I have convinced you that we have to remove the stress from the workplace. Bringing it home from the shop or cubicle and releasing it on loved ones should never be an option. Keeping it bottled up inside isn't good either, as it will result in health problems, which wind up affecting the nurses and doctors. People who are in this frazzled state too often settle in front of the tube in order to relax. I can assure you that even though people fall asleep watching reality TV and baseball, that medium was never – and more so today – meant to relax anyone.

Overworked people – any color collar or no collar at all – also turn to drugs for relief, many of which are illegal. I can't recommend the legal ones, even alcohol, nicotine and caffeine. None will help you in the long run. You may feel relieved or numb at first, but there will be bills and hell to pay later. You can see why we all need legislation for a thirty-hour workweek, an increase in the minimum wage and a boost in the salaries for the others.

16
Where did I find the time?

On many occasions I talk to retirees, and so many mention that they enjoy their new life and wished they had left the work force sooner. A few wonder where they ever found the time to actually have a full-time job. I asked the same question since I hung up my consulting shoes. If you are wondering, I only had a couple pair, but one contractor I knew had shoes to match every suit he wore. I recall he had a red suit, blue one and green one. He could wear any clothes he wanted since he was six-foot-five and weighed two hundred fifty pounds.

I finished writing my workaholics' guidebook in August 2001. On December 31st of that year, I retired because I felt that if I hadn't, I would have been a hypocrite. I had enough of the business world and now I just write about it. I'm retired without a paycheck, but for me, there aren't enough hours in the day. Somehow, I am a great deal happier and many people who took the identical route feel the same. Some never retire because they either love their work, the money or they wouldn't survive if they had no office to go to each day. The last two indicate a sad state of affairs, but you could retire and then wind up bored. There are too many individuals who wind up like that – they just can't cope with the free time. It is unfortunate that people can't relax and remove themselves from the rat race. I've known many people who fit this mold.

If I compare my life today to when I was schlepping off to Rochester on various contracts, a few things haven't changed that much. I still am involved with computer programming since I maintain my own web site. I haven't escaped email and the Internet – I wish I could. Even when I received a paycheck regularly from consulting, I was writing; now I'm still doing it but dedicating more time to my books. The good part is I don't worry about snow and commuting anymore. I also have a great deal less apprehension on Sunday evenings, as I need not worry about getting up the next day at some ungodly hour. The mileage on my car is much less than during my contracting times and that means less frustration on the highways. I don't miss any of that, at all.

Of course, no one can retire unless she plans it in some way. I mentioned the consultant who favored various-colored suits and matching shoes but I didn't know him that well. I did hear that he got the big bucks when he was doing his thing. He also had no qualms about spending either, so much so that he came back begging for another contract later when he ran out of funds. He violated one of the first rules of consulting: plan for days during a recession when there may not be work for a while. I saw a few of those stretches over the years.

Each of us needs to think about our future relative to retirement. This will mean using that finance tracker I discussed earlier. If a raise is forthcoming, you may not want to get out your credit card and buy that indoor swimming pool before you see the increase. Heck, even after you get your paycheck with more cash, you may want to consider paying down one of your credit cards instead of heading over to the bar and buying everyone drinks.

I'm not implying you should survive on a diet of red beans and rice. By the way, you can find a recipe for that dish in my cookbook. I like that combination of starch and protein, but you'll get sick of it if you have it day in and day out. Also remember that if you dine at fancy restaurants too often, it will postpone your retirement date. You could also get gout, a form of arthritis. I had a case of the latter in the summer of 2006, according to my doctor, although the symptoms resembled gout. You'll also be in the work force longer with overenthusiastic participation in Boxing Day. Perhaps I was blessed to get to the point where I absolutely abhor shopping. If you don't go out to the mall, you can always spend money by tuning in to the Shopping Network or going online, which I do, but sparingly.

You can read finance magazines that tell you when you can retire, based on your savings as well as your living habits. With little invested and living high off the hog, your retirement may not come for some time, even when you turn sixty-five. For quite a while I subscribed to *Changing Times* magazine, which then became *Kipplingers Personal Finance Magazine*. My only complaint – I cancelled the magazine a few months ago – was that it seemed to cater to the rich. Since the majority of the people aren't in that category, the publication may not be that useful for most of us.

Less than two years after exiting the business world – at least from a paying job – I sold my house. Materialism will hold down people so that they can't retire, especially when it comes to home ownership. Recently someone inquired if I missed the house and I said that I didn't. Obviously, there are aspects that I cared not to give up, but as is always the case, there are trade-offs. The home had three bedrooms but I could only recall one instance in which all the beds were used, including the sofa bed in the living room. That was after a party.

The house bordered an empty lot and I tried to buy that property but didn't succeed. When I sold the house, I realized that I really didn't need that extra land after all. People who buy 6,000 square feet homes might eventually feel the same way. The space might be nice, but you'll need furniture to fill those extra areas and your mortgage will be higher than for a smaller place. You'll also spend a great deal of time cleaning and maintaining the place or else opening your wallet to pay someone to do the work. All this will postpone your retirement.

What you collect can have a great impact on when you can leave your job. If you collect antiques – cars or furniture – you will need more room as well as more money. If you are into all the latest overrated high tech gadgets, the same applies and this can only mean a delay in retirement. One of the things I love to do is view movies, but I don't collect them. That's because I generally view a movie once since there are so many available. You may be able to get DVDs from the library and it won't cost a cent, unless you fail to return them on time. Buying means you'll have to work more to pay for the flicks but you'll also need more shelving to store them. That will cost you as well, unless you build it yourself, but then you'll have more work.

Spending something seemingly insignificant as a one-cent piece results in nickels, dimes and eventually dollars coming out of your wallet. You need not account for the pennies and nickels, but you have to worry about the dollars. I again emphasize the financial spreadsheet to monitor where the money goes.

As you can see, in order to retire, you need to think about it as soon as you enter the work force. I have already mentioned the Individual Retirement Account, which everyone should take advantage of, no excuses. If you are self-employed, you need to invest in Keoghs, profit sharing plans or whatever people call them. They have so many names, but they're nothing more than your own pension or retirement plan. If you are employed in a full-time position, you can only hope that your employer will take care of your future. Too often, people thought their employer was looking out for them after they turned sixty-five, but as corporations experienced tough times in keeping up the huge profit margins to pay off upper management and the shareholders, they felt the only option was rolling back benefits. As a result, employees lost some or all of their pension plan. This would have given them the benefits they deserved when they wanted them.

17

Nickel and dimed

The above three words are the beginning of the title of a book by Barbara Ehrenreich, who also wrote **Bait and Switch: the (Futile) Pursuit of the American Dream**. The full title of the companion book is **Nickel and Dimed: on Not Getting by in America**. Both works are hilarious and insightful and deal with work, the subject of this book. I highly recommend each. Dealing with the financial spreadsheet, I stated that you don't have to enter data to the penny; you can just enter dollar amounts. However, if you use credit card receipts and checks for the entries on this document, you already have the expenditure to the nearest cent, so why not use it? Besides, if you lose enough pennies, they add up to a dollar. I'm sorry for mentioning that so often, but it's definitely worth repeating.

You may have heard of the grocery store scam in the 1970s. If not, it happened when some creative checkout clerks used the subtotal key when they were doing their thing up front. Let's say that a customer with a full grocery cart followed another with a very small order. The worker would ring up the first order, but only subtotal it. The purchaser would pay for the goods and leave with her receipt. Then, when the larger order was calculated, the total would include the amount of the order preceding it – that which had been subtotaled.

The first amount may have only been two dollars, but the checkout clerk could pocket this amount and continue his thievery with more orders in the same manner, thus enhancing his wallet at the end of the day and ripping off the consumer. The customer with the large order probably wouldn't check to see if he had gotten ripped off. It was a grand old scheme, while it lasted. As you can guess, the subtotaling doesn't happen anymore. Now people get ripped off because of the missing intelligence of the help. Of course, computers can also be simply programmed to do robbing from time to time, and who would know the difference? In either case, the buyer pays more than he should have.

I went to the same grocery store twice within a two-week period and on each visit I was charged more for a few items than I should have been. Quite a while ago, I was charged some outrageous amount like seventy-nine cents for some shrimp that should have been $7.90. I didn't discover the undercharge until I got home and didn't report it. I also didn't go back to the store when I was overcharged recently on those two occasions. Eventually, all this probably evens out but I think by this time the food business owes me.

I generally don't check if the transaction is what it should be, but on many occasions I do a mental calculation at the register to get a rough idea of the bill – I did major in mathematics so that is not that difficult. Once in a while, I'm really close in my guess and not long ago, I came up with the exact amount – that's downright scary! On a few other occasions, my bill was more than I anticipated by a long shot. When I finally did the checking at home, in most cases my mental calculator just needed a battery, but every so often, I have paid more than I should have.

The same thing happens in department stores as we get nickel and dimed to death. By that I mean we pay more than we should. With technology the way it is, this shouldn't happen, but the people working behind the counter enter into the picture. Even if the computer is wrong, you have to be aware that it is programmed and controlled by humans, who can make mistakes, even if they happen to be honest ones.

Over the years, it seems to me that many businesses are making a living by overcharging for items. They figure that if the customer complains, they will reimburse him and apologize for the error. There's no harm done and they could even wind up with extra cash in the till. Actually, customers can stop frequenting these places and head over to a different store to make their purchase. That is what I recommend. On one occasion, I used my credit card at a service station for a repair and I was charged double. I fixed the problem by refusing to pay for any part of the bill and the merchant accepted that.

Pennies are important, but some people get really carried away because they are always counting them. These are the "humans" that can be classified simply as cheap. At the other end of the spectrum we can find those who spend every last cent they earn and more. I have known both classes of individual. You may want to avoid hanging out with either of these types. As in most things, we need a balance. The brilliant cerebral comedian, Steven Wright, pointed out that there's a fine line between fishing and standing on the dock looking like an idiot. Similarly, there is a small distinction between being a miser and being thrifty. Our job is to save money rather than go out of the way to save a nickel.

Some people will drive fifteen miles out of their way to save a dollar for gasoline. In the process, the gas they used cost two dollars, but they didn't calculate that. Then there is the individual who returns to the food store – which I didn't do – and gets a quarter refund because of an overcharge. Unfortunately, he gets home much later since the trip causes him to run out of gas. What about the "handyman" who decides to get his energy supply for his wood stove and buys a chainsaw to cut down some trees. In the process, he gets the wood but damages his house and winds up paying hundreds of dollars for the repair. His insurance doesn't cover bumbling lumberjacks!

We get nickel and dimed when people scam us and on too many occasions we would really be grateful if it only involved those few coins, but unfortunately it usually involves big bucks. This is going to be a really long story so you may want to get a beer. On second thought, make it a coffee, as I don't want you to fall asleep. I won't preview how it turns out so you will have to read all the way to the end of the episode.

Education that comes later is better than none at all or as they say, "Experience is the best teacher but it's a hell of a way to learn." In January 2005, I received an email from a Snidely Whiplash (not his real name.) He had been to my web site and thought that I could benefit by using his site to sell my books. I had to put information on his site about my books along with images of the covers. This would give others an opportunity to see and buy quantities of books from me, at a discount, of course. The fee was $340.

I have always believed in doing things big. Why sell books individually when it's much more beneficial to sell a hundred copies to someone else who then sells them for you, one at a time. You make less money per book, but in the process you sell more books and get more exposure. Overall, you wind up with more money in your pocket. Because of this feeling, I decided that his fee wasn't that much and figured that I would give it a try.

Snidely's company name was TYM, which now that I think of it stands for *Take Your Money*. I should have known better. I used my Borders Credit Card to charge the fee and proceeded to add the data necessary to the TYM site, including the images for my book covers. I had been on the phone a couple times with Snidely and he seemed decent enough. Unfortunately, I couldn't see his mustache because I didn't have a picture phone. That would have been another good clue.

A few days after my data was on TYM, I returned to the site and noticed that the images of the book covers were distorted and I figured, not ideal for selling books. I emailed my mustachioed business associate and mentioned this. He didn't respond so I sent another email. I got no reply so I called him but didn't talk to him, so I left a message. He didn't answer that message either. I was frustrated so I decided to log on to the TYM web site, figuring maybe someone remedied my problem. I made a mistake entering the web site name so I did a google search and what I found was very interesting. It was a list of complaints against TYM. You may be able to find some bad things about a company by doing just what I did. The Internet is not without flaws and lies, but there is a great deal of information that you can use to your advantage. Just do so before you get burned, not after, like I did.

At this point, I came to the conclusion that I had wasted my money. I checked out some of these complaints and these victims weren't happy either. I recalled my attempts to reach Snidely and I couldn't come to any conclusion other than that I had been scammed. I found the charge information for TYM on my credit card bill and saw a phone number for the company, so I dialed it. I got the message, "The person you are trying to reach is unavailable," and that was the end of the call. I thought that was peculiar. Wouldn't a phone that rang without stopping accomplish the same mission? It wouldn't cost as much or frustrate the caller, either.

I called the credit card people and related what had happened. I was told that I could get a refund provided TYM didn't live up to their part of the contract. I had to send some documentation, which I did and a few weeks later, the charge was reversed. There is justice in the world.

Unfortunately, when Snidely got the news that he was out $340, he was upset, so he took action. I didn't find out about his being annoyed until sometime in March. I was contacted by Chase Bank, which had taken over the Borders credit card – their real names. I was given a chance to prove my case to Chase, although I had done that, weeks ago. I did the Internet thing, got documentation and sent an email but was told that the stronger my case, the better chance I would have. I emailed more proof and got another response along the same line. I figured I would get more information and email it first thing the next day. By the time I got ready to send what I had, I was informed that the charge had once more been reversed, so I owed Chase a few dollars, $340 to be exact.

Now, not only was I upset with TYM, but with Chase as well. Through all the proceedings, I was forced to do unnecessary work, and I wasn't very happy. In the days that followed, I contacted the Attorney General, the Better Business Bureau (BBB) and Chase Bank, trying to establish my case. I even talked to my lawyer and he gave me the lowdown: it would cost me a hell of a lot more than $340 to win my case, no matter how good it was. Attorneys were of no use to me in this situation. I was down but not out but then I received the Chase credit card bill, even though the account wasn't active. I still don't like banks!

At first the bill was just $340, but then with each passing month, it started to grow, like the national debt. Interest and late fees were piling up while I continued writing letters and contacting people. I concluded that the BBB wouldn't help, nor would the attorney general. Nonetheless, I didn't give up. Contacting TYM was worthless because I figured I wouldn't be able to reach them. I tried before with no luck so why would it be any different now? In their fabrications to prove their case, which I happened to see, they had the nerve to state that though their response to me had been slow, they had lived up to their end of the contract. What response? To this very day I have yet to hear from them! Maybe the people at TYM are planning to go into politics.

In July, I saw a bit of hope in my Chase credit card statement. My bill had been reduced by $143 and I hadn't written them a check in months. It was a courtesy credit for being a good customer. I wrote another letter in early August to Chase, mentioning that were I to pay the remaining charge, I would be an accomplice to a crime, condoning rip-offs in the business world. I didn't use exactly those words, but you get the idea. In August 2005, my Chase credit bill arrived and it was zero and closed out. I had persevered and won, although not completely. I wasn't quite done with Snidely and TYM.

The lessons from my debacle should be obvious. Watch out for scams, do as much research and checking ahead of time as possible and don't give up. One person can make a difference. Of course, you can accomplish more with a group of people. Unfortunately, in some cases, you may have to do it on your own and worse still, you will have to spend time doing things that you really shouldn't have needed to do. You can't retire if you allow people to scam you.

Another individual gets ripped off by some con artist for $39 so he spends days and nights and tanks of gas to make things right. I'm sure that happens to most of us and even I have to admit that I was a victim, got upset and thought I'd do something about it. Eventually, I came to my senses and realized that it was only a few bucks and I would never recover the damage. People think of using the courts to settle matters, but the amount of return doesn't approximate the costs. They do it as a matter of principle, but meanwhile their principle is diminishing in their checking account. You may not even win the case and consider the time you have wasted.

All considerations have to include a realization that your time is involved in recovering what someone took from you. Maybe things were better when we were struggling to come up with cash for some special event. We seemed to be happier then, but changing times have something to do with that. If you don't have money, people can't rob you. Money may be the root of all evil, but we still need some to survive.

18
Art Vandelay

If you haven't already figured it out, I am a big fan of Seinfeld – the show and the comedian. Even before the program made it to the top, I felt that Jerry was an insightful comic and many of his observations were hysterical. Initially, the twenty-two minute program was just all right, but eventually, it soared. It reached a peak and then started on its decline, as the writing seemed tiresome and the creators seemed to be stretching to get a laugh. Maybe the writers just ran out of hilarious ideas. It was at this point that the decision was made to end the show. When the final episode aired, many were disappointed. On the contrary, I found that the conclusion was brilliant and an absolutely fitting end to the long-running series.

If you never saw the show, you have plenty of opportunities today. It runs in syndication on a host of stations and if you have cable, you may be able to see it four or five times a day, not that doing so is a good thing. I catch the program at times, but really don't have to worry about which episode I will watch since I taped the program. I don't have every half hour tryst, but I have most of the production, including the shows that featured the non-existent character Art Vandelay.

The reason I chose the title for this chapter is because I want to talk about art – the other kind, not Linkletter, Garfunkel, Donovan or Vandelay. This includes writing, music, drama, opera, ballet and Picasso and his friends, for starters. All those in this category work to make a living at their craft, but it's a real challenge. The same disparity in wages between the corporate head honchos and the workers can be found between the top artists and those that are waiting on tables and struggling to make a go of it.

You've heard too often the directive to those who want to be writers or musicians, "Don't quit your day job." This calling will limit you to action part-time, while forcing you to report to the office each day. If you already have a nine-hour day and come home to a family, there won't be much time or energy left to do any painting. That is why something needs to be done so we don't lose all the artists.

Not that long ago, we witnessed too many branch closings of the public libraries in Western New York. One library closing was too much for me to accept. I blame those in charge for the failure to keep these branches open. I expected them to do this as well as to do more to improve each unit of the system. A community that loses it art has lost its soul.

You might indicate that funds were just not there, but I don't accept that excuse. There's all kinds of grants available that should have been looked into and if they couldn't be obtained, it was the duty of management to somehow get funds from somewhere. If you can find DVDs, videos and CDs throughout the county libraries, this indicates that the money is there, so go get it. Not obtaining resources only indicates incompetence and no planning whatsoever.

Another gross injustice is cutting funding for the arts. You may argue that some of the stuff that passes for art shouldn't be awarded any encouragement at all, especially in the form of grants. Putting any limits on what should be subsidized and what shouldn't, goes completely against the idea of creativity, whether it's music, sculpture or writing. If we say sayonara to certain art, even the good, you may just as well say goodbye to civilization. Today, many large corporations give huge grants for starving writers and drug-infested musicians. Detoxification isn't cheap, but it is necessary.

There's no reason why funding needs to be cut at all. In fact, it really should be increased. If a country can waste vast sums of cash for defense – more than should ever be needed – then there is no reason why there should be a shortage of money for the arts. After 9/11, it was evident that our tax dollars were wasted since it looked as though "the defense" took the day off. Maybe people were too worried about the offense. I myself, found the leaders of the country to be quite offensive, but that's me.

If we want the arts – and we can't exist as a progressive society without them – we are going to have to put up with some mediocrity. With the good, comes the bad. We have television, don't we? Most of that "art" isn't funded at all and I can't see why it should ever be. It's about time that the people in charge of programming finally put quality ahead of greed and come up with some innovation soon. It's long overdue.

Over the last few years I have gotten familiar with many aspects of the writing profession. I need not tell you that the numbers of books available for you to read is endless. Unfortunately, with some of the great stuff comes a lot of trash. I read a lot, so I do have to put up with the good and bad. I eliminate some of the chaff when I pick out the books I want to read. Even then, I wind up with some junk from time to time. Some of these books are best sellers, too. That description only means that a book has been marketed and subsequently sold hundreds of thousands of copies. Hitting the million mark in sales doesn't mean that a book is good or even that many people have read it.

Generally, publishers don't help writers in a big way. The bottom line for them is what will sell. A book that has the potential to sell a million copies is what they are looking for – they don't want sentences ending in a preposition. To them, some standards – such as decency and the truth – are not all that important. I'm talking about the major publishers but the smaller ones also have the same outlook. There is another type of publisher that has gotten into the market: print on demand (POD.) These seem to be environmentally friendly as they only produce a copy of a book if someone wants it. The writer doesn't need to rent a storage unit for the thousands of books that his publisher makes him purchase after publication.

This latter type of publisher is how I got my first book published. Just as there are the high-standard royalty publishers and those with no concern for anything except making money – what I described first – the POD business also has companies to avoid. Unfortunately by the time you realize that your publisher isn't the best, it will be too late. I've had two publishers to date and expect to have a few more. As you can guess, I chose the second one because I wasn't all that pleased with the first. Don't worry, they won't read this – they didn't read the three books they published for me.

I have found that the most enjoyable part about writing is the actual sitting down to create a book. Successful marketing escapes me and I think it is even a puzzle for those who specialize in it. If they can't master the art, I don't expect to be able to either. Let me do the writing, get good reviews and I'll leave the rest up to the promoters.

When I worked at Nestle Foods – my first job in the business world – one of my bosses would give me record albums that he didn't like. I love all kinds of music, so I thanked him and listened to every disc. Many of them I thought were fine efforts and yet some of these artists never made it big. They had talent, but they missed the one ingredient for success: marketing. We have seen numerous examples of just this phenomenon. There are also cases where someone has no music talent or less and she still sells millions of copies of records.

Lauren Bacall was said to have no acting talent – I dispute that – she couldn't sing or dance and yet she brought people to the theatre – movie and Broadway stage. I can think of a few other performers who fit this category. It all has to do with the editing room, adding the right musical accompaniment or what have you and throwing in tons of promotion. Meanwhile, the artist who works hard and smart and has talent but doesn't get marketed, struggles to make ends meet.

The other concern for the artist is the reviewer. In early October 2006, I saw a group from New York City called the East Village Opera Company. Their performance was a fusion of rock and opera. Besides *Carmen* – I only stayed for the first half – *Jesus Christ Superstar,* and *Rock-a-bye Hamlet,* I have seen one opera in my life, *Andrea Chenier.* On various occasions, I have heard bits and pieces of operas since I do listen to classical music. That may be why throughout the performance of the East Village Opera Company, many of the selections sounded somewhat familiar.

The critic who reviewed the group from New York probably is as big a fan of rock as I am of opera. Actually, I think I like opera better than he loves rock. He panned the performance, despite the fact that the sparse crowd – me included – loved it. The crowd got so much into the show that this enthusiasm spread to the group on stage, who in turn contributed to the appreciation by giving their best effort. What I especially enjoyed was that you could see that the East Village Opera Company loved what they were doing.

If you are an artist, you have to be able to put up with the bad reviews – they will come every so often. If you get nine good reviews and one bad one, you're on the right track. On the other hand, if nine hate what you did and only one cares for it – even if it is your mom – you've got to regroup and you have work to do. Getting back to the rocking opera, I know the critic's name, but I don't know what he looks like, and my friend mentioned that he and his partner might have been the two people who left the performance early. I don't know, but if that was the case, he had no business doing the review. Too often someone will pan a movie or book but not see the flick or read the book. I am almost positive that I experienced this same review process for one of my books, although I can't prove it.

I mentioned favorable words for what you do as an artist, but I should caution you that too much praise isn't good either. You really shouldn't please everyone. If so, you are doing something wrong and you're not human. Chances are you won't have to worry about that happening. As you know, even great books and movies have been given crap reviews but people experiencing them have felt otherwise. Movie critics are no different from other reviewers. I have seen films that the reviewers raved about and I thought were less than average or worse. At the same time, I absolutely loved some of the flicks that they panned. This is to be expected since subjectivity enters into the equation in any review.

Artists are a part of our existence. Don't despair if you happen to be struggling as one. If your career seems to be stagnant, think of what your role is in society. However, it should be obvious that since this work has to be done on a part-time basis, it is imperative that two things are necessary today. First we need to implement the thirty-hour workweek. You know the other. We need to raise the minimum wage.

19

Bumps in the road

Speedbumps: Flooring it through Hollywood is the biography of the actress, Teri Garr. It's hysterical, informative and inspiring as I learned much about her of which I wasn't aware, including the fact that she has Multiple Sclerosis (MS.) However, she does not let this challenge stand in her way of living.

We, too, face obstacles in life, especially when related to work. Up to now, I have mentioned quite a few things that we aren't especially thrilled about in the corporate environment. A business that posts record profits and at the same time downsizes and outsources jobs probably won't have a position for you. It may not be a place you'd want to work anyway, even if you could find a job there.

I mentioned the oil companies before but might not have stated that besides moaning about losing money doing business, these corporations posted record profits. They were also on the receiving end of tax write-offs and subsidies. Giving people money when they don't need it isn't good for the economy and the gouging continues. Driving through the inner city on too many occasions, I can't help but notice that gas prices are always higher there than in other areas nearby. If it walks like a quail and talks like a quail, it probably is a quail, even if a person shoots at someone else.

A company that doesn't allow the workers to unionize is not my kind of place. This is especially true of companies that pay their employees the minimum wage and ban the formation of unions. It gets much worse as a company does quite well financially, hires mostly part-time help so that it can avoid paying benefits like vacation pay and health insurance. When an employee cannot even afford to shop at the place she works, maybe it's time for all shoppers to go somewhere else.

Unions were formed because of the horrible working conditions and long hours imposed on those on the job. Given the similar conditions that exist today, it appears that it's time for a resurgence in them once again. If a company treats its workers so well that that the laborers are content, then the unions aren't needed. Unfortunately, the vast difference in pay between the CEOs and the employees is so great, the working conditions so pathetic and the hours so long, that the unions are the only way that the companies can be brought to do the right thing.

People will argue that we can't have the resurrection of the labor union because of all the corruption that took place during the twentieth century. Are their practices any worse than what we are witnessing today on the part of corporate America? You've heard of the major scandals over the last quarter century, so I won't bore you by listing them. Each day we hear more and more about sleaze in the business world, brought about by companies from whom we purchased goods.

We hear about recalls every day for automobiles, appliances and electronic goods. That is not encouraging but in a way is much better than not being informed of these problems. The alternative I have already discussed earlier: keep the people in the dark and pay the lawsuits. Still, pride in workmanship as well as better quality control can eliminate many of these problems.

I don't have to remind you of our "service" economy. This is the new business model where we replace those who answer phones with "voice maze," or maybe I should properly refer to it as, "voice malaise." Whenever I hear these words, "Your call is very important to us," I want to add, "But obviously not that important." Too many times you can't get through to any human being about your problem. In many cases you wander through the menus only to eventually hear, "Thank you for calling," followed by a dial tone. This is the new way of doing business.

There seems to be a simple word for these efforts: greed. This uniting of people in order to do unethical things is nothing more than a conspiracy. If you haven't figured it out, I believe in them since conspiracies aren't theories, they're CRIMES! Just such a travesty occurred on October 17, 2006 when a judge reversed the conviction of Enron founder Ken Lay, turning over a jury's verdict that he had committed fraud and conspiracy in one of the largest scandals in history. This decision was most likely made because Mr. Lay died a few months before. I believe in forgiveness, but do you think the victims of Enron's theft will be able to feel the same since this outrageous judgment means that they will never recover any of their losses? Actually, the judge wiped out a conviction because the defendant could not appeal the decision – a good thing in case someone is falsely accused.

In my view, there is just one problem with this recent decision. The deceased had an attorney to file an appeal in the event that it was needed, so why was this ruling necessary at all? You may have heard about the person who faked dying and then crawled off to the Cayman Islands to retire without using his social security benefits. This is another example of a conspiracy since I doubt that the perpetrator could have done it alone. Just because something is legal does not make it ethical.

If someone is found guilty of robbing the people, not only should he be put in jail – have fun with Bubba, dude – he should also be made to restore to the victims whatever was stolen. There should be no provision made to protect any part of his estate, whether we are talking about residences, gold, paintings or Bibles. There are laws to protect the possessions of criminals, but they are obsolete and should be thrown out. Everyone has rights including the innocent victims. I think we can trust those in the courtroom to do the right thing where those involved in these cases are concerned.

Tort reform is another big joke to protect the criminal corporations. Who cares what the amount of any lawsuit happens to be? Don't we have judges and juries to limit payments if the claim is excessive? If so, then why is there any need for reform in this regard? All it does is protect the companies for their irresponsible actions. I'm sure you've heard about the destruction of the environment by these thieves. These are the entities that have been treated as citizens. They have the same rights except they don't want to be bothered by responsibilities. The sad part is that the Environmental Puke on Americans (EPA), Department of Environment Corruption (DEC), Don't Overlook Hallucinogens (DOH), Can't Provide Anything (CPA) in Iraq – you may have thought that the acronym stood for Coalition Provisional Authority – and other organizations of the government either are too shorthanded to be effective or they just don't have any concern for the citizens of the country.

Another pet peeve of mine, which you know about already and I can't emphasize enough, is doing stuff that really isn't necessary. One blaring example is what the Congress passes off as work, showing they deserve the salaries that they get: introducing legislation. I pointed out that we already have plenty of laws and don't need more. The Patriot Act wasn't needed and only reduces the rights of the citizens, which our government was supposed to protect. Before it was passed, there was enough legislation already on the books to handle any scenario that resulted. Another example of wasted time has to do with flag burning. Since there is a statute about not starting fires in public places, why do we even have to introduce any bill for flaming flags? Unfortunately, these redundancies happen every day in congress.

Some will disagree with me about my feelings about the Patriot Act and tell me that if I have nothing to hide, why should I worry about someone looking into the books I read. On a trip to Maine in September 2006, I only took a single book, ***Where the Money Was*** by Willie Sutton and Edward Linn. I'm not planning to rob any banks or anything else for that matter, but when I left the motel room, I did hide the book in my overnight bag so that the cleaning lady didn't report me to the authorities. This should point out the lunacy of the Patriot Act. It's amazing and quite ironic that the administration that believes in this piece of legislation is the most secret government in history. Benjamin Franklin said it best: "Those who sacrifice freedom for safety deserve neither."

For a society to exist, it needs laws. If a country has none, the only thing that will result is chaos. On the other hand, too many laws mean that they won't be able to be enforced and the result is noncompliance or rebellion. Obviously there needs to be some rules, but there is a limit. You can't have too few precepts nor too many. That middle ground will result in a successful society that most will accept and be happy with.

Despite the promise of our legislators – trusting them is like believing that the eighteenth century Native Americans and the colonists were buddies – we know of the huge failure of NAFTA and the World Trade Organization (WTO.) If you want a few good laughs, view the movie, *The Yes Men*. The heroes of the movie created their own web site called GATT.ORG. It appears to be legitimate, but it's a huge scam – one I like. Nonetheless, there was a method to the creators' madness. They wanted to have some fun and make a statement at the same time. This web site did fool some individuals and the duo was asked to give some presentations at various meetings of the WTO. What these two came up with was outrageous, hilarious and very enlightening. What was more unbelievable was the acceptance by those in the audience of the ludicrous ideas presented. This is where the title of the movie originates and we all need laughs to survive the daily challenges in the workplace.

In the summer of 2006, I sent off a manuscript to my agent about the failure of technology, *Press 1 for Pig Latin*. In the last chapter, I mention that there is something that we can do to correct the problem. There are so many reasons why our lives are so messed up by technology. It doesn't take a genius to see that it should have made our workweek shorter but it has done just the opposite, and hence the huge failure. If I am blaming management and corporate America for our predicament, you can see that I have very good reasons. They are a huge factor in our arriving at this point.

Just consider email. When I got my first email address, I was quite excited by the possibilities of this new type of communication. As I write this today, I realize that I was hallucinating since it never came anywhere close to what was promised. I need only remind you of spam, viruses, spyware, emails with FW (forward, not the middle initial of someone preceded by the first letter of another word) in the title and racist, degrading jokes that you see over and over. Don't forget the replies that you are expecting which never come as well as all the promises that you and your entire family will be turned into circus people – not that there's anything wrong with that, but what if you're scared of heights and they ask you to be a trapeze guy – if you don't pass on the email.

In a two-year period, I changed my Yahoo email address twice. The first was necessary since I was getting bombarded with obscene overtures, having nothing to do with music – I didn't open them but the subject title gave that away. More recently, I did another change because I was getting about thirty junk emails each day. With my current address, I'm getting a couple daily, but many of these are for mortgages. I can't figure out how anyone got my name for this possibility since I haven't had a home loan for years now and I have no intention to buy a house.

I was at a family reunion in the summer of 2006 and one individual argued that email was a great thing. In this case, we seem to have an exception, but remember, I had that same feeling initially. Email was created to keep everyone connected and promised instant communication. Unfortunately, the designers forgot about the fact that some people only check their messages every three months. They also didn't take into consideration that every transmission doesn't take place. I have sent emails that people have not received and simultaneously have not gotten stuff that others have directed to me. It's possible these correspondences were accidentally or otherwise deleted, or perhaps the sender didn't press *send*, but it still points out the flaws of the system.

Email is a one-way communication. Certainly spam fits that category as does just about any other piece you get with FW in the subject title. You can't respond to spam, but if you open it, beware! I don't keep track of responses to the emails I send for which I want a reply and I don't pass on FW emails and jokes, unless they're really hilarious. If I did keep track, I am sure that the rate of returning mail is very low, probably about five percent, if not less. I recall one specific occasion when I emailed someone, who didn't reply. I needed an answer so I resent the email. At this point the recipient told me to stop my spamming! When I got that message, I didn't respond, figuring this person wasn't worthy of any more of my time.

This new creation was supposed to help us be more productive, but now we wind up keeping lists of people and spend time maintaining more than one. When someone goes on vacation, on her return, she will have to spend hours checking the messages that have accumulated. This applies at home as well as at the office. Yahoo has an option to direct your email into the inbox or the bulk folder – another name for spam. It somehow determines which is which, but every so often, I will get spam in my inbox and good mail in the bulk folder.

Yahoo – your provider might do the same – offers the option to have the junk deleted and go directly into the spamopshere and you'll never see it. There is another option that goes with this, giving you a chance to save the email addresses of all this crap so you can see who the sender was. In doing this you might find that Uncle Leo emailed you but it was deleted instantaneously. Maybe that was really what you wanted, but you can see the problem if you were a favorite niece of the guy, who was loaded – money, not alcohol. As far as I can tell, this last option doesn't seem to function properly since I tried it and no email addresses were saved so I could send a correspondence and request another email from the sender. You may just as well have the separation of the mail and look at them all before deleting. In any case, you can see all the work that has been created. Do you still feel that email is all that great?

There are a few things that can be done to make email what it was supposed to be. The elimination of this junk "correspondence" will go a long way to another goal: improving communication by this means. No one has talked about this so maybe it's time for some email etiquette. Here are the rules that should be put into practice:

1. Each individual is limited to sending one email per day to each recipient.

If you send an email and get one back and then decide to follow up with another to this person on the same day, it's time to pick up the phone.

2. No Ponzi schemes of any kind are allowed.

Avoid sending stuff with a threat that they will have to sit with an insurance salesman for the entire afternoon if they don't pass on what you sent to ten others.

3. If you plan to send jokes or humor of any kind, make sure it's funny, not racist, sexist or condescending and above all, get new material.

If there won't be laughs without these considerations, don't send it. You can always pick on politicians, lawyers, agents and businessmen – they're still fair game until they clean up their acts. On too many occasions, I get the same funny material over and over and it's old stuff – some of which I included in my books or unpublished manuscripts. Either this person didn't read that book or he is a speed reader – he reads without comprehension.

4. An email with no subject should never be sent.

If the title is "no subject," it appears that you have nothing to transmit, so don't send it.

5. A greeting and signature is always an example of civility, so use them both and avoid emails that are one word or less.

You really don't need to send just the two words, "Thank you." If you really feel you should, add a bit more to the message. I get many emails without the names of the sender. Should I reply, "Hi no name or senior moment person?"

6. Don't send epics.

People don't care to read long, boring emails so keep it short and to the point. If you go on and on, you are not being concise and people won't read what you sent. I certainly won't.

7. If you get an email demanding a response, answer it.

Why have an email address, if you are not going to check to see what is in your inbox, so you can reply? Above all, don't wait three months to respond. Perhaps it would be better not to give out your address if you have no intention of answering. Checking your email three times a year is not very considerate.

8. If someone emails you with something that isn't too nice, don't respond.

Answering means you have crawled into the gutter with the sender. If you still feel you must respond, wait at least a day before doing so.

9. Don't send links or FWs.

If you have to send the latter, at least go to the *subject* and remove those two letters.

10. Do unto others as you would have them do unto you.

On October 12, 2006, Western New York was on the receiving end of some snow, because of the unusual falling temperatures. From what someone told me, the people who bought my house got about five inches. Others weren't so blessed as they saw over twenty inches of the white stuff. The problem was that the snow was extremely heavy and leaves hadn't departed the trees. This resulted in power outages and almost unheard of damage to oaks and maples. Some individuals didn't lose electricity at all, while others were without it for days or even weeks. Within two or three days, the snow was gone. After two weeks, most but not everyone had power. The damage to the hardwoods was still around in many places for months.

Someone mentioned that this event was our Katrina or our tsunami. They weren't even close as this event was an inconvenience of the smallest order. The temperature rose on the days that followed so that very few were troubled by the cold. What was illustrated was the fact that we rely too much on technology. It failed us for those few hours and yet many panicked. How could they watch *Survivor* or *As the Stomach Turns*? There were some creative people who figured out they could watch their DVDs by going to their own cars or those of their friends or parents. Meanwhile, the non-vegan mothers and fathers of these geniuses wondered how to keep meat in the freezer from spoiling as well as how to preserve the dryness of their basements without a functioning sump pump.

Besides these natural disasters that are bumps in the road, I should also add a few words on another thorn in our sides: the Political Action Committee (PAC.) They haven't helped the people and their contributions to our plight are as damaging as any factor. It does not appear that we can move away from eventual erasing of the middle class unless these leeches are destroyed or at least regulated so that America can progress to a more just society. It's time to bring the poor into the middle class so that both can advance. Let the rich – at least those who just accumulate wealth and do nothing for others – contribute to arrive at a more sustainable, equitable society.

You can see what the obstacles are that we face in our daily living. Big business doesn't seem to help either the worker or the consumer and yet wants people to buy their goods. If there is not a soul to bring out the product because management is overworking the help to death, how can the goods get to the market? If you expect the government to solve any of your problems, you will have a long, long wait. All three branches seem to be on permanent vacation. I've sent letters to my representatives and on many occasions received nothing in reply. When something was forthcoming from a representative or senator, it merely thanked me for my input but ignored my suggestions anyway.

We, the people, don't really have the time or energy to do other people's jobs. With all the hours just trying to put food on the table, we're exhausted as is. You won't feel like going to a meeting of the town board. Joining grassroots organizations is fine, but who has time to do it? That may be another plot of the bad guys, whether corporations or politicians. If the citizenry is too busy, the rulers and CEOs can carry on business as usual (BAU) – a phrase I really hate – doing whatever they care to do in their quest for riches and power.

In this way, we are slaves since we can't assert ourselves. This has been going on for years and it is an example of the perpetrator using all kinds of tools. Drugs and alcohol enter into the equation. Being tired or depressed may lead to cracking open a beer or two, and in this state, our attitude may be one of procrastination, maybe even a permanent one. If you want to control a group, why not sell them some kind of narcotic – legal or otherwise? This has added benefits as you not only get to have people in the palm of your hand, but you can also make a few bucks on the deal. It's obvious that the possibilities are almost endless here: nicotine, caffeine, alcohol, illegal drugs and legal drugs. This is what you call a captive audience!

Assuming ordinary folks don't get hooked on dope or anything else, they shouldn't excuse themselves since they may be part of the problem. After all, corporations are made up of individuals who are human beings. The same is said of PACs, law firms, the government, and all its agencies. At times people resign good-paying jobs because the organization that pays them is corrupt beyond belief. I applaud these people and I also send out kudos to those in the business world who leave their offices for good and realize there is a better way to live. Despite all the bumps and potholes in the road, there is hope.

20

My pothole adventures

I received some information in the mail about a lawsuit. I'm the plaintiff – one of many – for a possible whopping payoff of $45 – actually it's more like $20 and a $25 E-store credit, whatever that is. The company is Epson, and it appears that for some time the software indicated to the printer that the cartridges were empty when there actually was more ink inside. Of course, the customer had to do a replacement at this time. This small scam meant more bucks for the company since more print cartridges had to be purchased. I doubt that I'll be getting another Epson printer. I probably will never see the refund, as small as it is, since I responded to this rip-off over four months ago.

I had planned to relate another appropriate incident in which I was involved that stretched out over a few years but decided to not do that for security reasons: my own. Let me just say that I saw a great deal of incompetence – that shouldn't give you any clue to the company – followed by what I thought was a shady, if not illegal practice. I signed a document that would give me some cash – it wasn't in the millions or even hundreds of thousands, but it was substantial – in return for saying nothing about the situation to anyone. My vagueness here should cover me, but I will talk to my attorney before publication.

This deal occurs every day when businesses settle out of court but then refuse to accept any blame for what happened. There seems to be billions in payoffs for all this incompetence and criminality. How can businesses survive that way? The power is in the hands of these giant corporations, so much so that we the people have no chance at all to do more than get a few dollars from them while they proceed on their evil ways. In my case I could have refused the money and not signed the release, but not only may no reprimand or fine resulted for the situation, I could have been out the payment completely. It could have been worse if I had been offered a pair of concrete shoes, which don't match any of my suits. Unfortunately, this is what we see every day in the way companies run their businesses.

I was visiting friends in Mississippi a few years ago when my friend John mentioned a news flash on the Internet about the town of our youth, Bellevue. My parents' home was downwind and less than two miles from this area in Cheektowaga, a suburb of Buffalo. It seems that there was a huge lawsuit against some of the businesses there for destroying the environment and getting the residents sick. Cancer, asthma and autoimmune diseases were way above was what was expected from a neighborhood.

The list of defendants was quite lengthy and as it turned out, there were to be about three hundred plaintiffs. My sister, Pat, and I were both involved because of our cancers, and in 2006, my brother – he had lived at that same house during his teenage years – also had a bout with cancer. Fortunately, we are all survivors – so far. The major polluters and possible cause of all the sickness and death are a stone quarry, an asphalt plant and a few landfills. You might think that the plaintiffs weren't alone as the lawyers, politicians and government organizations such as the DEC, EPA and DOH could step in to help us. We had a great case and legal representation, but the law firm eventually backed out of the case for lack of funds and the other support became as useful as having W teach a course in balancing budgets.

It boiled down to staying the course – that reference was accidental – without legal representation, which would have been three hundred separate hearings against the defendants. That would have worked in our favor because the judge would probably have demanded some kind of settlement on the part of the toxic trespassers since she simply didn't have enough time for that many cases. However, by this time many had dropped out of the lawsuit – coffins aren't allowed in the court – and now we were stuck with a handful, about thirty or less. This didn't help us at all and eventually the lawsuit was dropped.

The reason why so many people gave up had to do with the feeling that they couldn't fight city hall, if you know what I mean. It would have been different if the people there – in city hall, or in this case, the town hall – had been on our side. That's another story. Other plaintiffs lost interest because they were too sick to even think about going through this lengthy process. In all, it dragged on for over two years before we saw the disappointing conclusion. Both of these reasons are understandable and the latter may be part of the strategy of the caustic corporations. If you kill off the people or at least get them sick, they won't have the energy to react in any meaningful way. At the time of the litigation, I was in good health, despite everything that had passed, but after a while even I got disgusted and tired. How do you think those with really serious illnesses felt? The law may say that companies have to follow regulations, but if they are not policed, do you think they give a hoot?

Recently I was informed that the Norton Anti-virus Protection software for my PC (Piece of Crap) had expired and needed to be renewed. I had a few options. I could go online and take care of this. I could also call an 800 number, which is what I did. The whole transaction was a bit fuzzy but I do remember being given an update option for about $50, but being warned that I should probably get the 2006 version of Norton Anti-virus, which would set me back about $60. Either choice seemed a bit excessive but I decided to stay current and asked for the more expensive alternative. I was told that I couldn't order it at that moment since their system was down. I was asked to call back later, which I agreed to do.

I did some thinking and realized that maybe there was a better option. I checked out the Sunday bombardment of ads in the paper and discovered that a few places had the same software for $39. The ad indicated that with a mail-in rebate, the software would be free. That sounded too good to be true and it was a much better deal than what I had been offered, so I picked up the product at Office Depot. While buying the software I mentioned to the checkout person that I could have had the same deal for $60, with no rebate. Why would Symantec – the maker of this fine software charge so much when I could get it for nothing?

As is true with most rebates, there was a waiting period of six weeks or so, but after doing the requisite mailing, I did get an email saying that my claim was received and the $20 dollar rebate would be processed shortly. You might think that praise is due for the marriage of Office Depot and Symantec for this excellent deal. As you can see if you've done the arithmetic and were paying attention, the refund should have been almost double that since $39 - $20 does not equal FREE! I'm somewhat happy to report that I did receive a check for $20 after about six weeks. It's possible that Symantec offered the $20 and Office Depot was to kick in an instant rebate of $19 to affect the full rebate, but as you can see that didn't happen. According to my dictionary, this sounds like a conspiracy.

How can customers believe that this Anti-virus software isn't a huge scam? I run it every week or so and week in and week out, I see the message after it is done, "There are no threats found." That is a good sign, which means either the software is working or it's really not needed. I'm not sure which option applies here, but if it is the latter, I just wasted $19. I would have been happier with a $39 rebate so I could care less about a scam by Symantec. This also seems to apply to all the other software on your PC (Positively Crud) such as spy ware and fire walls.

I figured that I would never see the $19 but I called the store where I bought the software, anyway. It turns out that you had to mail in two – not one – rebate things to get the full refund. One was a green label attached to the box that Norton Anti-virus came in, which was nowhere to be found on what I brought home from the store. I was quite pleased since the person I talked to was very helpful and offered a way for me to obtain the rest of the rebate, which I actually pursued. In my mind, Office Depot may have been off the hook, but I can't say the same for Symantec and I was waiting for the rest of the rebate, when I received a postcard stating that my request was denied because the original proof of purchase was missing. I was almost ready to resign and do nothing further, but then I saw an 800 number on the card and I decided to call – what could it hurt? After suffering through voice maze I finally got a human on the line in a far-off country. I mentioned to him that they had the required document since I had sent it in months ago and he said that my rebate check would be mailed within four to six weeks.

On December 8, 2006, I received a letter from Symantec and thought that I had my check, but they sent a plastic thing with Visa written on it. At first I thought it was another credit card – which I really don't need – but it was actually a debit card in the amount of twenty dollars. Surprisingly, the refund arrived within two weeks. Symantec thanked me for being a customer and added these words, "We have decided to offer you this rebate method so you can instantly use your reward without having to make a trip to the bank." Apparently they are unaware that I cash my checks at the pawnshop.

From this episode, I give Office Depot and Symantec two huge thumbs down – even though my name is neither Roger nor Richard, but it does start with an "R." For the two people I talked to at Office Depot and Symantec, I give praise because of their efforts, without which I wouldn't have gotten the full rebate. Of course, I would have been a great deal happier if there had been an instant rebate, without the need for mailing anything. My choice would have been to get to the checkout and be told that I owed $5. This scenario is not the exception but rather the normal way big business is done. I mentioned BAU before but maybe it should be Crooked As Usual (CAU.)

If you really want to head down a road loaded with potholes, try being a writer. Besides bumps in the road, there are huge crevasses, at times. I even wrote a book about those adventures in my third profession, *I Don't Want to Be a Pirate,* but that's another story. My agent has that manuscript, too.

One thing writers do is sign books, sometimes even at bookstores. On the evening of the last day of September in 2005, I was part of a group of local writers at the Barnes & Noble store on Niagara Falls Boulevard in Buffalo. In an hour and a half, I sold six books – not bad for an evening's work. What wasn't too great was the fact that I brought the books in myself and for each book sold, was only to receive 60% of the cost of the book – that at least was my impression. You may think that's not bad but don't forget, I paid the publisher for the books in the first place.

Authors were encouraged to tell their friends, family and groupies about this event to fill the store with customers. The thought was that with so many people congregating at the tables, other people would drift over to see what the buzz was all about and may even buy a book or two. Maybe they were giving away cheesecake. I didn't tell many people since I figured that my friends didn't like dessert, they either had my books or they could buy them from me, increasing my profit. I also felt that too many people congregating might actually get in the way of buyers, something the store didn't consider.

People that bought books took their purchase to a register and paid the list price of the book, plus tax. How many books each writer sold was done by an inventory check with each writer before and after. Prior to the event, each book identification or ISBN was entered into the store system. B & N got paid for the sales that very night. You might feel that the authors should have gotten paid at the same time, but are you ever dreaming! Allow at least a week for payment, but I was more pessimistic and gave them a month or two.

I am a patient person – although not that thrilled about being a patient in the hospital – but in February 2006, more than four months later, I had still not received the check for the sales of these books. I called Dawn, the woman in charge that September evening and she said that there had been a snafu, which she would handle. After a few more weeks I still hadn't gotten the check so I emailed her, but there was no response. I emailed again with the same result. Then I composed a letter to corporate headquarters of the company, getting the address from their web site. In it, I demanded the full cost of the books since I had to wait so long. That made no difference so I contacted Diane Newton, a friend who also sold a few books that night. I included a copy of the letter to her and she advised me that I needed to include the ISBNs for each book. When I talked to her, Diane mentioned that she got paid for her sales a few months after the event.

By this time I felt that headquarters should have contacted the store here and verified my claim and the ISBNs should not have entered into the picture. Anyway, I redid my letter, including sending a copy to the local store, but all these efforts proved futile. At this point I figured it might be better to end this caper and forget about the profit for that evening. I could have avoided all this had I been a prophet.

Sometimes, someone smiles down and looks after you because on one Sunday, I saw a feature in the Buffalo News by Karen Robinson, a woman who writes a column handling complaints by consumers against corporipoffAmerica. I emailed her about my predicament and within a few days she called. A day later I spoke to a B & N company representative, Mary Ellen Keating, who wanted to settle the matter as quickly as possible. I guess you could say we had her "sweating bullets" – which would come in handy at the gun club. It might be more accurate to say that this was Karen's doing, since my efforts until this point had been completely futile, as I mentioned.

Ms. Keating mentioned that there had been a screw-up, but no one was to blame. What? Do I have to forget everything I learned in logic class? Well, I can tell you who was to blame. First, the local people were culprits because they knew that the writers had to get paid, within a reasonable amount of time and they didn't take care of getting at least one check sent. I got the corporate address from their web site, so if it was incorrect, the main office messed up. Since I wound up sending three letters, corporate headquarters gets blamed again. Certainly Cliff Claven may not be the best government worker, but from my experience, the mail does eventually get delivered with great regularity. Granted, it may arrive mashed, crushed, pureed, mangled and broken, but at least you receive the gist of what was sent. I think I would still have been able to cash the check.

A day after talking to Mary Ellen, by overnight mail, I got a check for the entire amount of my book sales. In addition, there was a one hundred dollar gift card. From that September evening, B & N should have gotten $15.27 from the sales of what I wrote – I later discovered they took merely twenty percent of sales. Instead they wound up paying approximately $120 for their screw-ups.

I was grateful to Karen, so I sent her thanks and the following Sunday, my letter was in the business section of the paper with how it was resolved. Somehow the article seemed to exonerate the company, especially after such a long wait. It wound up being settled in June 2006, over eight months after the book signing. The headline was, "Barnes & Noble more than makes up for delayed payment." I can only conclude that Karen either has a relative working at B & N or else Ms. Keating agreed to settle the matter, throwing in a $100 bonus if Karen agreed to have it sound like the store should be recommended to consumers.

Needless to say, I used the bonus and bought a few books, but how can I recommend this store to anyone? I won't shop there and probably won't get involved in any more of those book signing evenings there. This last decision is based on the fact that this caper gets even worse, even before it started. Diane, who I mentioned earlier, another writer from the Authors Guild of Western New York, emailed me news of this event about a month before it was to take place. At first I thought I wouldn't get involved because of past experiences with this store, but then

I thought that even if I sold nothing, I would get some exposure – not that kind, I'm not that type of person.

I called Rene, the woman who was in charge but didn't talk to her. Instead I talked to Dawn and she said that she was doing the event and would call me the next day. I'm not sure what she considers to be a "day," but a week passed and I heard nothing from her. A week later I phoned again and she told me to be patient and she would get back to me soon. Another week passed but she failed to contact me.

By this time, it was getting close to the event and when I reached her, she mentioned that all the slots for authors were filled. I was furious but stayed calm on the phone with her, becoming even more determined. She said that there could be cancellations. I then asked if she wanted me to drop off my latest book and she said that would be fine. My house is nearby, so I stopped in with the book but she was at a meeting. Managers spend too much time at those things rather than working. I gave the book to someone who said she would deliver it.

The next day, I called Dawn again and asked if she got the book and she thanked me for taking the trouble. She also mentioned that no one had bowed out of the event but I just said that I would still be there with my books, despite no writer withdrawals. She then stated that she wouldn't have a flyer for me and I wouldn't be listed in the program but I told her that was not a problem; thus I became part of the night. I'm sure I sold more books there than some of the people in the program.

I mentioned my apprehension at first because I also got involved there on a similar evening the year before. On that occasion, I managed to sell no books. Two years before, I had given my books along with contact information – including my address, email address and phone number to Rene. She didn't contact me and when I reached her by phone, it turned out I wasn't part of the agenda. Why she didn't contact me I don't know. Maybe I should have sent her some Godiva chocolates!

21
Grocery freedom

The only way to avoid doing the grocery thing in obtaining food is to marry someone who loves shopping – I'm sure you can find people like that. However, then you will probably cry because that person spends too much of your paycheck. There seems to be no solution to this dilemma. Well, I think there are a few things that can be done to make food-finding fiascos far more favorable. Obviously, we can't do it alone and will need some help.

The stores have to pitch in. They can start by not accepting coupons. Simply lower prices on items. Another great idea is to get rid of those bonus cards that fill up our wallets. I will return to those cards shortly. Buffalo has two main players in the grocery business and a few smaller companies trying to keep pace. The big guys are Tops and Wegmans. The former has an awful reputation, which I can attest to from the feelings of others as well as from my own visits to their stores. That wasn't always the case. Wegmans is somewhat better and even one of the top 500 companies – whatever that means – which they like to brag about, but I really find that difficult to believe from my experiences with them. Maybe I just have a bad attitude from all those days when I worked at the supermarket all through college.

Now the two major players just brag how much better they are than the other. Instead of bickering like politicians before an election, why not simply show results in your store. Actions always speak louder than words. Wegmans and Tops seemed better for the customer years ago. On one occasion, I walked into one of the two places – I can't remember which one and it doesn't really matter – and asked a clerk if they had gumbo file, a necessary ingredient for making Creole dishes. Actually, it's nothing more than ground sassafras leaves, but what a flavor it adds. That store didn't have it, but the individual I talked to suggested I try their competitor, right around the corner. I thought that this bit of assistance was a really great thing, above and beyond the call of duty. They satisfied my needs even if I had to head into another store. I found it on the shelves of the grocery store just recommended and was really impressed by this civilized gesture.

As far as those bonus cards go, they are a big joke and not needed. At one time you could have used them to get into your apartment if you lost your key, but today they are not even good for doing that. About a year ago Tops closed one of their massive stores, remodeled it and re-opened it under the name, *Martins*. I went to the store, did some dreaded shopping, went to the checkout and handed over my Tops card, but the checkout person said that it was no good there. You might think that I lost all those discounts but that didn't happen. Instead, the clerk got a generic card, processed it for my order and I had those savings, implying that the card never was necessary in the first place. I went back to the store on another occasion or two, but did not get one of the cards for the store. It wasn't many months later that Tops reappeared and *Martins* was history, at least at that location.

This same scenario plays out any time you shop at either store. Just tell the checkout person that you left your card home. They will accommodate you and you'll still get all the lower prices. I have been asked for my card to be used for another customer ahead of me, but I refuse to give it to the cashier – I don't want to get into trouble. Of course, I'm kidding, as we shoppers are all in this together. Nevertheless, you probably won't be blessed with the discounts if you don't say anything about leaving the bonus card home. The clerk usually is kind enough to ask for the card if you forget to bring it out. When Tops first instituted the cards so many years ago, someone roamed the store asking if you applied for the card. This assured that all the consumers were on an even keel; but as I pointed out, you could have shopped for months in the store – nay, years – obtained the benefits without ever enrolling in the system.

All the card does is create two prices for many items: the regular one and the discounted value. Executives say this process was carried out because shoppers' trends and shopping habits were needed for marketing purposes. I ask, "For what reason?" Save a few dollars on promotions, get rid of those cards and the result will be more contented people in the store and more business, which is the bottom line. I have too many cards in my wallet as is.

We have been blessed today with the superstores. As far as I am concerned, even the large stores cover too much ground and you can never find anything without a safari. I get more exercise than I need when I shop. It's nice to have a great deal of choices in making purchases but I'd be more content to know where everything happens to be. You can master where each item is by limiting your venues to a single place or two; but wouldn't you know it, just when you think you had a handle on where everything is supposed to be, someone moves things around. I think that effort is a huge plot to keep us in the store longer. They figure we'll buy more stuff, or at least pay them for the opportunity to find our way out of the joint.

Every store has at least ten checkouts, but when people are trying to pay for their stuff and head home, only two or three are open. It's rare that you see every checkout open, but why not open more lanes if shoppers are backed up down the aisles? The answer invariably is that there's not enough help. Well, wake up some of the stock clerks in the back room or do some hiring. The latter option will help the employment problem – somewhat – and result in happier customers. That translates into better business. It doesn't take Einstein to reach that conclusion.

You will also see shopping carts large enough to buy groceries for the entire army in Iraq. It's good to have roomy carts but they also block up the aisles. Any family that needs that much room for groceries may want to consider the South Beach diet or move there, if such a place exists. I believe – with minor exceptions – that the smaller wagons should give you sufficient room. Another phenomenon is the circus cart – created to entertain the spoiled brats. Some kids even get their own tiny vehicle, which I'm sure you've seen. How quaint! Are children so out of control that these devices have to take up room in the aisles just to calm them? Haven't parents heard about Ritalin and Dexedrine? I will allow for the motorized carts for the handicapped, but not the other vehicles.

This gets me to one aspect over which management has little control: road rage in the grocery store. It's not really that bad but sometimes I really want to ask customers if they drive that way on the highway. Fortunately, I keep my mouth shut – it's hard to talk that way – so they don't run me over. On one occasion in the fall of 2006, my mouth wasn't open but that didn't help in the least as a woman ran me down. I'm exaggerating – one of the wheels of her cart touched my foot, so it was no big deal. It didn't hurt at all, and she did apologize. I assured her I had another foot, to which she smiled.

None of the employees can do much about the aisle hogs. These are the ones with the big carts who park on one side of the row and then stand right in front of their carriage looking for chocolate covered ants, effectively blocking off the way and you can't get around them. Actually, a small cart can achieve the same effect. If the stock clerks are filling the shelves, they can also do their part to add to the congestion. When I did my thing stocking shelves, I usually worked on less busy evenings or early in the morning, like midnight to nine a.m. – the graveyard shift. Those were fun if you liked being a zombie!

Today, with very few supermarkets not being open twenty-four hours a day, there probably won't be a time when the store doesn't have customers. Fortunately, the wee hours of the morning are appropriate for the help to load the shelves with cans and bottles since customers at that wretched hour will either be minimal or so inebriated that they won't see the employees. The problem can easily be solved as mentioned earlier in this book by closing on Sunday as well as during these times when decent people should be sleeping. The workers can still stock the shelves during those bewitching hours, because from my experience, they're not decent.

I could go into some of my recent grocery gathering adventures, but instead let me talk about some ideas for management. They probably shouldn't hire someone who can't tell the difference between bananas and summer squash. I know: they're both yellow, at least the one kind of squash. After a time, the help should learn the difference between leaf lettuce and romaine, just from repetition. I was at Wegmans one day, and was charged for Chinese cabbage and mushrooms. That day, I had neither fungus in my cart nor anything Asian. If you are checking out a customer – that's not the way I mean – and don't know what an article is, ask the buyer. There is a very good chance he'll know what it is. She may even be able to tell you the code of the fruit.

One annoying aspect of life is that tiny tag that you find on fruit from the supermarket. Having read this far, I'm sure you have a fairly good idea of where those tags belong! Those stickers do come in handy for the clerks since all she – in my day, there were only female checkers – has to do is punch in the code. In fact, with bar codes and entering the cash handed the checker – assuming he can read – there isn't much that can be messed up in the process. I like to really confuse those people behind the terminal by handing over unusual amounts of cash that would give me quarters back for the laundromat. I don't do that now since I use my credit card for purchases, but I still need the change for the wash.

I was about to advocate that employees have some basic skills in math but that really isn't necessary with today's computers at the front of the store. Everything is done for them except taking breaks. Nevertheless, being able to do a bit of addition, subtraction or multiplication wouldn't hurt, especially during a power outage, when these basic skills could come in handy if the store remains open. This alternative I have seen at Wegmans on occasion and my hat goes off to them for giving people the chance to shop, even if it might be too dark in the store to read the labels on the products. I hope they don't pick up a summer squash when the missus wants bananas, but that's why we have night-vision goggles.

When I compare shopping for food today with the time I bagged groceries, chased grocery carts and stocked shelves, it appears that a great deal of progress hasn't taken place. In my workdays, we did our best to get the shoppers away from the checkout and on their way home as quickly as possible, something that doesn't happen much today. This is despite the fact that the advances in technology should lead to shorter times checking out. Years ago, we didn't have unit pricing and the cost of every item had to be input and sometimes wise-ass shoppers handed the clerk $11.23 for a $10.73 bill because he needed change for the washer and dryer.

A few things that I see every time I shop could be eliminated. Invariably, I will be asked if I found everything I was looking for. I might answer in the negative, but that's the last of the conversation. So, why even bring it up? Also, when I purchase bottled aqua – I go through it like water – the individual who checks me out puts a sticker on the top of the gallon container to show that I didn't use a five-finger discount. For those of you not familiar with that method of shopping, read Helene Stapinski's *Five Finger Discount: A Crooked Family History*, an entertaining, sometimes hysterical biography of the maturing of a journalist, growing up in New Jersey. That added tag for the water seems a bit redundant since I have a receipt to verify that

I am not a thief, at least of that liquid. Perhaps, this person has stock in a paper company. I like to save the forest as much as possible. Another thing that you are always asked is, "Paper or plastic?" Isn't there another choice? Actually, there is an answer to that dumb question. If you can, bring in your own cloth bags. You'll have fewer bags to carry and you will help save resources and the environment. The only challenge you might face is lugging the bag outside the store since the bagger managed to get everything into it. I guess it's better than seven plastic bags for six items!

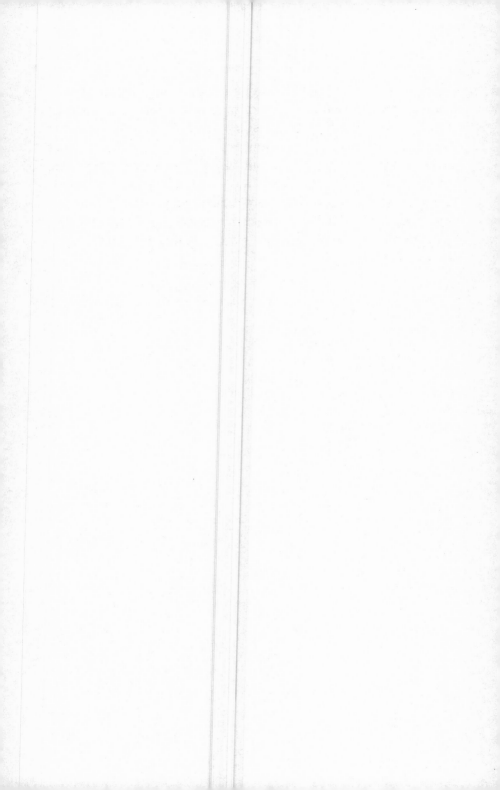

22

Can he run again?

I realize that as I write this, the president of the United States can only serve two terms in office. Does that mean that George W. Bush can be on the ballot again in 2008 since he really hasn't served the majority of Americans? Granted, he has catered to the rich, but I don't think that counts. If you have been awake during the twenty-first century, you might feel that the Congress hasn't earned the pay raises that they approved for themselves in the middle of the night. This lack of effort on the part of our rulers does not help the people of the land. That is why those in the middle class or at the poverty level have such a tough time.

The government has failed big time and so have their agencies, some of which I have already mentioned. Favor the Elite but not the Majority of Americans (FEMA) should return their paychecks and they still would owe us. I mentioned writing those in the Senate and House of Representatives earlier. These are activities that I engage in that I really should not have to do. I am forced to proceed because others have not done their job – something that we the people pay them to do, through our taxes.

I should not have to write someone in Washington to see to it that the minimum wage is increased so that people can have food on the table and a decent place to live. I also shouldn't have to tell my representatives that the idea of going to a conventional war to fight something quite unconventional as terrorism might not be the right thing to do. I shouldn't have to write my senators to do something that is ethical and makes sense, and give a laundry list of why something should be done or avoided.

When people mention that politicians are not serving the populace and it's time for a change, but still reelect their representatives, I only hope that these individuals are people who deserve to be elected. Unfortunately, if everyone in the country feels the same way and elects those in the neighborhood, the slime will remain. The situation won't ever change. If the elected fail in their duties – as I write this, the Congress has an approval rating of 20%, so that says something – boot them out and give someone else a chance. If the newly-voted-in are also below par, another election will be forthcoming and they can be removed as well.

Unfortunately, it's not who votes that counts but who counts the votes, as the last two presidential elections point out. If you think both were on the up and up, you need to read *A Black Way of Seeing: From Liberty to Freedom* by Paul Robeson, Jr. If I have to tell you who his father was, you're not reading enough books. Turn your television off for a few hours. You can also read *Was the 2004 Presidential Election Stolen? Exit Polls, Election Fraud and the Official Count* by Steven Freeman and Joel Bleifuss, as it's always nice to get a second opinion, even though the verdict is the same. All we can hope for is that this never happens again, but don't hold your breath.

Along with others, I blame the wimp Democrats for allowing this to occur. At least Al Gore put up a fight, but others could have said something after the final decision was made on who would be president after that election. In 2004, one clear indication of foul play was the result from the exit polls, which showed Kerry to clearly be the winner. These type of polls are quite indicative of the winner in an election and there's a lot more chilling testimony in the Freeman / Bleifuss book.

If you didn't skip history class – although from some of the books that are still used in the schools, doing so may not have been a bad idea – I'm sure you are aware of the system of checks and balances. The three branches of the government police each other. How do you have a just society when laws are passed and the president signs them but then decides not to follow them? George W. Bush has done this on quite a few occasions with signing statements, an attachment to a piece of legislation that indicates disagreement. Boston Globe writer Charlie Savage mentions that W has used this device 750 times during his tenure. This is not the first time that signing statements have been employed, but others have used them very sparingly, especially before the Reagan siesta. As far as I am concerned, why not just veto the bill, something until recently that the president "elected" in 2000 and 2004 hadn't done in six years. Maybe this wasn't done because the veto could and probably would be overridden.

I thought that we had a branch of government to check the powers of the other branches. There wasn't much monitoring before heading off into another war in Iraq in March 2003. Apparently, politicians figured that they might be considered traitors if they exercised their rights and duties by questioning the idea of this unjust, unnecessary and illogical war. If you start with the premise that war should be avoided at all costs, you can't help but come to the conclusion that a doubt here can save a hell of a lot of money over the years if conflict can be avoided. If no thinking or debate on the issue is held, you'll be sorry later.

You may have heard of King George and it appears as though he's back. Unfortunately, I was under the impression that we lived in a democracy and weren't especially fond of dictators. In the summer of 2006, you probably heard a great deal of noise about fascism from the people in power in Washington. Well, they got that right, but they were talking about themselves. It seems that our capitalistic society has evolved into the "F' agenda. Webster defines fascism as "a political philosophy, movement or regime that exalts nation and race and stands for a centralized autocratic government headed by a dictatorial leader, severe economic and social regimentation, and forcible suppression of opposition."

You can blame anyone you like, but you won't do badly by faulting all three branches. I might also add that the ink-stained wretches, i.e. the media, went on vacation too. At one time we had great journalists. I need only mention Ernie Pyle, Walter Cronkite, and my favorite, Edward R. Murrow. I also think that we still have great people in the press today, but many were silenced over the last few years. Here I am chastising the incompetents who cared only about collecting a paycheck and had no concern about integrity. This describes too many of people in the media. If you are not familiar with how the press has let down the public, read **Watchdogs of Democracy? the Waning Washington Press Corps and How It Has Failed the Public** by the great dean of the White House press corps, Helen Thomas. Bush booted her out of the staged press conferences because she asked too many good questions. She's the real hero, and I hope you understand the question mark in her title.

I might add a few more accomplishments of those who serve us in the Nation's capital in this decade. There's the huge national debt and then we can't forget the tax cuts for the richest Americans, but squat for the people that really could use it. I stand corrected: *squat* should be *pennies*. This maneuver took place during "war time," something usually not done.

Long after I wrote this chapter, I asked myself if it really belonged in the book. As you can tell, it's all about a really nasty business, politics. A while ago I emailed a friend something, which had to do with that same agenda but the response was that he didn't get involved in that raunchy realm. Those weren't the exact words used – you know I'm embellishing, here – but I think you have an idea of his feelings on the situation. Well, I told him that he couldn't ignore what was happening and each of us has to participate, even though we know that most elected officials are crooks. Actually, there are some good ones, but you wouldn't know that from all the scandals and the way the country is being run today.

You may not be a candidate for public office at any level – although I wouldn't discourage you if you felt the calling – but as a citizen, you need to vote. One of the reasons for much of the mess today is the failure of people going to the polls in recent elections. A country that sees less than 50% of the population exercising its right to vote is on the way to disintegration. Also, it is much more difficult to rig an election if 80% of the people get to the polls.

Many people don't participate because either they feel that their vote doesn't count or they aren't familiar with the candidates. Many are turned off – myself included – by all the filth in the campaigns. The dirt can be eliminated in some way by sending messages to those who employ those underhanded, sleazy tactics that they just won't be elected. Every vote counts, or at least it should and you won't know who to favor if you aren't familiar with the candidates. This means you have to do some homework before the election – but don't worry, you won't be graded on it. Obviously, you won't agree with everything a politician says or plans to do if elected, but one person running should have enough of what you believe in to earn your support. You also shouldn't base your choice of a candidate on a single issue. Each of us needs to do our part. Things won't improve if we are apathetic. Of course, working more than one job and having to labor for fifty hours a week for pennies won't allow us the opportunity to study any political race. That's the dilemma.

23
Get up and dance

One of my favorite episodes of Seinfeld was the show that found Kramer's degenerate friend making a bootleg movie, which I found hilarious. You may not have heard that Cosmo is part of the new comedy team of Borat and Kramer. For that laugh, I thank my friend JJ in Minneapolis. There was another storyline in that same episode in which Elaine started up the party by dancing, or an unreasonable facsimile thereof. Our female star had the guts to get up on the dance floor and we should do the same. It really doesn't matter if we can boogie or not. Eventually, we'll learn and get better.

I complained about some pet peeves of mine, and you can see that all seem to be tied in to "work." We go to school to be able to get a "good job," which as I pointed out is an oxymoron. Too many people are hung up on careers, when all that really is necessary is to make a living and be able to retire at a reasonable time. To do that, one must get an education, but to be able to go to school, someone has to pay for it and that falls on the family. Most of us are not blessed with the resources to be able to attend classes without getting part-time employment. You just can't glide through the process by being on campus in the dorms – they're gone now but that's what the out-of-town students lived at in my days in college. Attending the university today is a huge financial challenge for the majority of students, even with scholarships. Just buying overpriced textbooks will require getting a part-time job. Paying for education will require monthly payments for some time once graduation day passes.

To be able to have dough – I'm not talking about bread, although that's slang for what's necessary, but the green stuff

– you will have to work, or you could follow the career path of Willie Sutton. I have already mentioned his book, which should entertain you as well as inform. Willie "The Actor" Sutton was an exemplary thief, something that can't be said of crooks today. For a few laughs at thieves behaving without brains, check out the 2001 movie, *Big Trouble*, based on a book by columnist Dave Barry. For a humorous look at missing intelligence, especially "criminal behavior," pick up a copy of my book, *for seeing eye dogs only*, which was published in July 2005. In the summer of 2006, I sent another manuscript of similar material to my agent. There is so much stupidity in the land – exemplified by our Nation's Capitol – that I am already collecting material for a third book on temporary brain deficiencies.

If you are into changing your address often and love garage sales, you must realize that you won't be able to get involved in either without cash, which once more means you need to work. Of course, you can be excused from that preoccupation by inheriting huge sums of money or by gambling. It is a possibility for people to not have to work, provided they are lucky. You may not want to actually believe that buying lottery tickets can replace getting a job. If you feel otherwise, I recommend reading my novel about the national lottery, *Don't Bet On It*, published in 2003.

Any way you look at it – unless you are blessed with hand-me-down bucks – you are going to have to work. You can't escape that reality. Fortunately, there are possibilities to go through life without having to suffer all the stress that comes with the 9-5 grind, which unfortunately has "evolved" into 24/7 service and never-ending work. As I have pointed out, society is set up so that the richest people do the least amount of work while those who labor the longest and the hardest, get paid peanuts and these people are the ones who prefer pretzels.

I mentioned many obstacles in the way, but I alluded to the unfortunate baccalaureate procurers who face a double whammy upon graduation. If they go on to higher education, there will come a time when they will face the prospect of actually getting a real job. This can really be a hassle, especially when graduates have Stafford loans to settle. Moving into a job outside one's field or getting a position with inadequate pay only means that life will be quite a challenge making ends meet for these new entrants to the work force.

The correlation between stress, work and a good family life should be obvious and I pointed out that many workaholics really never cared for that way of life in the first place. It gets worse when one ism leads to others, which then leads to sickness and numerous hospital visits. The human race is in a spider's web and not only can people not exit the maze, the arachnid's trap gets deeper and stronger. Yet, we have to do something to change this circle, which has turned quite vicious.

Throughout the previous chapters, I have offered a few suggestions. What follows in this chapter should summarize what I have already pointed out as well as supplemental suggestions that I made in my other book on work. There are numerous things that we can do individually to improve our lives and get to the point where we can retire sooner. This is only done because today we have too much stress, which in turn causes health problems and if we are fortunate enough to be able to retire, we should be people who get a chance to enjoy those years away from the rat race in the best of health. As should be obvious, it will take effort by each of us to achieve that goal.

Since the press, unions, government and corporations are made up of individuals, we the people are part of the problem but fortunately, can help in accomplishing the solution. I have mentioned the need to keep track of expenses as a way to control them by the EXCEL spreadsheet. A few other financial choices that we shouldn't ignore have to do with credit cards and mortgages. If you carry a balance on your plastic for too long a time, you are only asking for trouble and you will have to work a lot of overtime. That extra cash still may not pay down those cards. A better idea is to control your spending and don't buy everything in sight. You'll need a place to put it! Use some discretion – it will enable you to retire sooner.

Also, materialism is way overrated, as is owning a home. Why buy a 10,000 square-foot place as a residence if you live alone or with only your loved one? If it's necessary because you moved away and need it for when your family visits, and you have plenty of brothers and sisters, motels are always a possibility and the sofa bed and a few extra beds in a bedroom or two should do the trick in many cases. Have people bring tents – the outdoors are really invigorating and guests can still have bathroom privileges if they set up in your back yard.

That big house means more cleaning, more furniture to fill it and a longer time to pay for the goods. It implies a bigger mortgage as well, which you really don't need. It is also more likely to get robbed than a smaller, humbler abode. Your goal to retire sooner is to pay down your mortgage as soon as is humanly possible, without having to do jail time for embezzlement. Granted, the meals there could save you money, but you have to think about your new associates, of whom you probably won't approve and may have some different habits than your friends and family. You really don't want to be sent away to decide if it is the place for you.

In order to get to be the exclusive owner of your home, consider adding a bigger payment each month for the mortgage. If your payment is $500, send $550. This will mean two things: you'll reduce the times you have to make payments and you'll pay less interest. It's true, eventually you'll have less of a tax deduction, but no one wants a hundred-year mortgage, even if the banks are dumb enough to offer them – yeah, they are that stupid. The interest alone for that period will mean your grandchildren won't be able to retire either!

You should also consider the painless bi-monthly mortgage, if your bank offers it. Instead of making $500 payments twelve times a year, you wind up with twenty-four of $250. As you can see, you pay the same amount, but write more checks and your mortgage is paid off sooner. To hasten the process further, add a few more dollars in each bi-monthly payment. Scratching and straining to do this will reward you with an earlier departure from the rat race.

24

It's time for a new band

We can get up and dance – which I recommended in the previous chapter – but sometimes the people responsible for the music should realize that they shouldn't have given up piano or singing lessons, especially when we can't gong them. Those responsible for the band or orchestra for our pleasure need to be kicked off the stage and replaced. Unfortunately, that may not always be possible, so they have to be advised about what measures to take. It seems that a few groups have been playing music that we the audience aren't exactly happy with.

Corporat America – since I'm missing a vowel, maybe I should contact Vanna – has to change its practices. What I have already put forth about the product / laborer connection can't be emphasized enough. Creating an outstanding product and having the work force to get the goods out to the consumer accomplishes one thing: the company will be a success and that will keep the stockholders happy. What more can you ask?

Studies have shown that outsourcing and downsizing simply don't work. If that's the case, why are these still being practiced? We need new solutions and a variation on downsizing should be employed. This one gets rid of the dead wood in a place, the non-productive people. More benefit can be gained by reducing the exorbitant salaries of upper management as well as slimming down the thick wallets of the CEOs – another form of downsizing for the better. Too much weight in the butt area isn't healthy as illustrated by George Costanza in one of the episodes of Seinfeld. Individuals should be able to survive on a salary of a few hundred thousand rather than so many millions!

The chasm between the pay of CEOs and the people who actually do the work is obscene and needs to be addressed. I have discussed the huge disparity between the Simon Legrees and the imprisoned lowly laborer so much but the gap is only increased when you throw in stock options and other perks. The CEOs can still have their high salaries, but let's level the playing field here. Perhaps it's about time to raise taxes for those who have so much money and roll it back to the people. This gesture will do much to boost the economy. History has shown that enacting tax cuts for the rich is never financially beneficial to the country. On the other hand, tax relief for the workingman will help the workers and the economy. Anyone with butter beans for brains can figure that out.

Since there is a limit on the low end, it's time for one on the high end too. No one deserves or should be paid a salary in the seven-digit range, which includes benefits – decimal points don't count in this discussion. Let us set a limit of six, as far as the digits go. I'm talking here specifically about athletes, entertainers, news anchors and CEOs and they will have to pay more taxes. They will still have plenty to live on but if their yearly salaries get to be more than a million bucks, they will have to write a check for even more to Uncle Sam. This "incentive" should make people realize that five hundred thousand might be enough for one year.

The corporations that have left the country need to be highly taxed rather than given tax credits. If you want to incorporate in Bermuda, that's fine but it will cost you and forget about any payola to stay in the United States. The penalty for moving should be so great that corporations won't even think of leaving a location for other areas to do business. The criminal oil corporations shouldn't be given exemptions so that they can pile more cash into their pockets by gouging the public while the latter struggle to fill up their gas tanks.

Companies need to be accountable for polluting the planet. If you pollute, not only do you have to pay for the cleanup, you will also be heavily fined. Repeat the crime and you do the time. In addition you will be made to pay even higher fines as well as clean up the mess you made. This change in the way business is carried on should keep the air, land and water cleaner and the inhabitants of the earth will also benefit with less sickness. This in turn means that the health care people will not be overstressed with work, since there will be fewer patients in the hospitals.

I hope I have convinced you of the lunacy of the fifty-hour workweek. Even forty hours should be replaced with a new maximum thirty-hour period for that same time frame. It's just common sense, something that seems to be in short supply today in corporate America. I spent over a quarter of a century in the business world and saw too many examples of what shouldn't be done there. The only good thing I can say for my experience is that it gave me plenty of material for books. Nevertheless, I would be a great deal happier if I didn't have to report on all these deficiencies.

I should also talk about overtime. Not long ago some workers were reclassified as managers so as to give corporations the option of not having to pay them extra for working beyond the call of duty. This is grossly unfair and I recommend that along with the thirty-hour maximum, we also set a five-hour limit to the amount of overtime one can put in during each week. The pay will be double the hourly wage of the employee and this would help out those who have been abandoned by the corporations over the years. Salaried workers would also receive the same consideration and compensation.

One of the great ideas that has been implemented at some companies is the ability of the workers to buy stock in their own place of work. This is a fantastic idea because it makes the company better as well as the work force, and it lets those who labor share in the progress and future of the corporation, as well as in the financial gains. Perhaps the retirement plan should be tied in to the company's success and this might eliminate some of the losses that investors suffered when the Enrons and Global Crossings tanked.

The fair minimum wage has to be implemented. If you still aren't convinced, why do some many businesses now pay nine or ten bucks an hour for the help. That magic number of fifteen is certainly doable. Don't worry where the money will come from as I have already pointed out the huge profits at corporations despite the downsizing and outsourcing at those same establishments as well as the bursting wallets of the overpaid upper management people. Taxes and fines for mismanagement and fraud can be used to fill the void. By the same token, since the workers will be rewarded in such a manner, it is up to them to earn their paycheck.

Paying a minimum wage of fifteen dollars an hour indicates that management needs to keep track of the help so that people are productive. Hiring the right people is a no brainer – that's why you interview prospective employees. If do-nothings are employed, you have to fire not only the sloth but the manager who hired him as well. Telecommuting, true flex time and the four-day workweek should be a normal way of doing business. This will help morale, increase productivity and reduce movement of workers to other jobs. If you have good workers – which you should have because of competent managers – you certainly don't want to lose them.

Corpoorate America – this is the term for the companies that complain about losing money while reaping huge profits – needs a huge restructuring as far as technology goes. If you are going to have Automated Phone Systems (APS), make sure that the process doesn't frustrate the callers and drive them away. If you can't figure out how to make the system user-friendly, simply go back to the old way of communication, which many businesses still use. You may think the automated system saves money, but it won't if consumers abandon the business. The first clue that your phone handler isn't working is if people think the acronym stands for **A**gitated **P**eople **S**creaming.

Technology needs a huge revamping. First of all, it has to be made user-friendly. Many people are into the process, but you shouldn't have to be a nerd to take part since we can't exist by avoiding what's there. The second improvement that is needed is to eliminate all the bugs in the software. I cannot understand how any programmer would accept a paycheck with all the defects in what he produces. Isn't management watching what's going on? Also, how can any company put out a product with so many deficiencies? Some people call these things challenges, but I call them bugs. A book could be written about all these problems, and having been there as a software consultant as well as having endured – and continue to suffer the defects of PCs and the Internet as I write this – I have done just that. The manuscript has been submitted to my agent and I can only hope that it gets published before the new millennium.

It is time to come up with some innovation and replace the mouse and **windows** with processes that all will welcome, no matter what age, and eliminate crashes, restarts and calls to the help desk – have your credit card handy! I included what follows in my manuscript of my experiences as a writer, which I hope to get published soon. You've probably seen it in emails, but it's worth another look.

At a recent computer expo, Bill Gates reportedly compared the computer industry with the auto industry and stated: "If GM had kept up with technology like the computer industry has, we would all be driving twenty-five dollar cars that got 1000 miles to the gallon."

In response to Bill's comments, General Motors issued a press release stating the following: "If GM had developed technology like Microsoft, we would be driving cars with the following characteristics:

1. *For no reason whatsoever, your car would crash twice a day.*
2. *Every time they repainted the lines on the road, you would have to buy a new car.*

3. *Occasionally, your car would die on the freeway for no reason, and you would accept this, restart, and drive on.*

4. *Occasionally, executing a maneuver such as a left turn would cause your car to shut down and refuse to restart; in which case you would have to reinstall the engine.*

5. *Only one person at a time could use the car, unless you bought 'Car95' or 'CarNT.' Then you would have to buy more seats.*

6. *Macintosh would make a car that was powered by the sun, was more reliable, five times as fast, and twice as easy to drive, but would only run on five percent of the roads.*

7. *The oil, water, temperature, and alternator warning lights would be replaced by a single 'general car fault' warning light.*

8. *New seats would force everyone to have the same butt size.*

9. *The airbag system would say 'Are you sure?' before going off.*

10. *Occasionally, for no reason whatsoever, your car would lock you out and refuse to let you in until you simultaneously lifted the door handle, turned the key and grabbed hold of the radio antenna.*

11. *GM would require all car buyers to also purchase a deluxe set of Rand McNally road maps (now a GM subsidiary), even though they neither need them nor want them. Attempting to delete this option would immediately cause the car's performance to diminish by 50 per cent or more.*

12. *Every time GM introduced a new model, car buyers would have to learn how to drive all over again because none of the controls would operate in the same manner as the old car.*

I couldn't agree more! As you can see from these points, Apple, Microsoft and GM – and they're not the only ones – need to get with the program. Changing the way they conduct business will go a long way to making all of our lives better. It will also increase profits for the corporations. How many times do I need to point that out? Does corporate America have the intelligence of a rutabaga?

Technology needs revamping since it has such great potential. Unfortunately, it is a major contributor to the increased hours of the workweek. Advances are supposed to make the week of the laborer shorter, but the computer companies are responsible for just the opposite effect. Take advantage of the possibilities, but get rid of the problems. Once this is achieved, corporate America can use the improvements to lower the workweek further. This gesture would also make our lives easier when we log on to the web to surf or get our email.

I spent a great deal of time on email and all its headaches earlier, but the Internet service providers can be more responsible to make our lives easier. It will take effort on their part, but spam can be eliminated, with a bit of enforcement and policing. I realize that spy ware and viruses create jobs. However, you can create some other jobs that will remove all these annoying hazards completely from our lives forever. It can be done and the people will be eternally grateful. I know I will.

With the state of affairs of what we the people are going through as workers, it appears as though it is time to bring back the unions. It wouldn't have been necessary had corporations dealt with their employees in a caring manner. The whole idea of forming these types of groups may be avoided if somehow companies make some changes. It really would be better for everyone, since any color collar workers – and those without collars – would save on dues and have more for groceries. Management would save time since they wouldn't have to do any negotiating, except with those whom they hired.

However, since management hasn't treated the help that well, it looks like the unions are needed. Economists Lisa Lynch of Tufts University and Sandra Black of the Federal Reserve Bank point out that studies show that American factories that are unionized and utilize the methods of participation and profit sharing for employees, such as those at the Saturn Plant in

Spring Hill, Tennessee, are twenty percent more productive than the average similar company.

It's is up to those in government to do their part to justify their exorbitant salaries, rather than sit around taking kickbacks from the political action committees, which I have already mentioned. I have written and emailed members of Congress with suggestions and comments and either have been ignored or thanked for my correspondence. However, no action was taken on what I offered, even though I justified what I was writing using common sense. Perhaps that was the problem. Still, all these attempts on my part would have been unnecessary if senators and representatives were simply doing their job and serving the people that elected them to office.

Politicians also have a part to play as far as social security goes – because of its uncertainty, some people have referred to it as so-so security. There are a few things that can be done to remedy the situation. First, grant all the people the same coverage that the Congress currently receives. The second suggestion is to eliminate what those in Washington, DC get now and replace their benefits with what the average American is blessed with. Instead of either possibility, I would suggest a compromise where both legislators and those governed receive appropriate compensation to live out their retirement years in a worthy lifestyle. It would also be appropriate to have the same outlook for health insurance.

Speaking of cash-coveting corporations and politicians who want to get on a different page, some of their members feel that global warming is a huge hoax. At least one of them is of the opinion that rising temperatures aren't really that bad. In a short time, we'll be able to grow bananas in Buffalo along with the yellow squash. These individuals will be extremely happy when St. Peter turns them away at the pearly gates – I should add that it's a dry heat.

Because people are so busy with their jobs and their lives, they really don't have time to sit down and write those in government, whether at the local, state or federal level. However, since they have the right to vote, they can and should vote out of office those individuals who only care about their own pockets and political futures. That's what democracy is all about. It is also up to the people, whether in political parties or those of us who vote for them, to see to it that everyone qualified to vote can do so. We must also make sure these votes are counted and done so correctly.

Maybe it's time for the people of this nation to form a new organization, using the same acronym I mentioned earlier. The organization I'm referring to is People Against Corruption (PAC.) I was at a party and someone mentioned that we have to accept payoffs, bribes and crooked politicians, since they exist and we will always have them. I don't buy that and you shouldn't either. It may take some time, but we need to demand that our representatives serve each of us. If they don't, they will only be in office for one term. It is our right and our duty as citizens to remove these deadbeats and bloodsucking leeches from office.

I mentioned my trip in 2006 to the state of Maine. It's a beautiful state and it is also responsible for the Clean Elections Act, which allows candidates running for office an alternative to the corrupt practice of campaign financing. Arizona and a handful of other states have also joined in on the procedure, which was featured in a 2006 broadcast of the NPR program NOW with David Brancaccio. Five-dollar contributions are accepted but no big money. So far, the results are so encouraging that I think more states should use it. For more information, do a google on "Clean Elections Act."

Two days before the election in 2006, I watched the highly entertaining flick, *Welcome to Mooseport*. Gene Hackman and Ray Romano are the two candidates for mayor of the town in the title after the incumbent dies in office. The movie gets into politics and all that goes with it, but it also underlies the fact that there is good in everyone. Best of all, it illustrates that everyone's vote counts. If you don't think one person can make a difference, you haven't heard of Rosa Parks, Paul Rusesabagina or Rudy Acuna.

The press needs to be more responsible. I mentioned Helen Thomas earlier and you may also want to get a hold of her 1999 book, *Front Row at the White House: My Life and Times* which describes her life covering presidents and dealing with press secretaries and First Ladies. Most important of all, this book confirms the fact that members of the press don't keep regular hours. Thomas took a lot of criticism for just doing her job the way it should be done.

There is good news as the Woodwards and Bernsteins are still with us today. In fact, we have a new team from that same paper, the Washington Post. Their names are Scott Higham and Robert O'Harrow and they reported on the overspending at the Department of Homeland Security in a weekly program on public television called, *America's Investigative Reports*. The amount of your tax dollars that was frittered away was seven hundred million dollars. The duo determined that this was money that was misspent and abused and, in some cases, involved fraud.

Unfortunately, it is almost impossible for any journalist to do any serious reporting that isn't tied to sensationalism, Hollywood or anniversaries that really shouldn't be celebrated. It has to be infotainment. Laura Poitras spent eight months in Iraq reporting on the elections there and she made the documentary film, *My Country, My Country*. She risked her life doing this, but it seems that she may be in just as much danger in the United States because she carried out this project. Apparently her production isn't exactly what the government wanted any American citizen to view.

I watched the movie and thought it was outstanding. I am in awe of anyone who does dangerous and courageous work of this kind. There are others who carry on just like her and I really support them, as well as some charities, since they are in need of our help. Collecting money for many organizations is necessary today because of cutbacks over the years. You may find it difficult to decide which groups that ask you for contributions are legitimate. Some are downright scams, while others mean well but spend too much on administrative costs. The remaining charities are those for which you may want to open your wallet. You can get help for making decisions in liberating your earnings by going to the web sites, www.charitynavigator.com & www. charitywatch.com.

Not long ago, I received an email with a bit of information, which I thought I should pass on to others. Marsha J. Evans, President and CEO of the American Red Cross received a salary for the year ending on June 3, 2003 of $651,957, plus expenses. Brian Gallagher, President of the United Way receives a $375,000 base salary, plus numerous expense benefits. The Salvation Army's Commissioner, Todd Bassett receives a salary of only $13,000 per year plus housing for managing this $2 billion dollar organization.

Someone will say that my ideas about minimum wage and the length of the workweek aren't plausible because it will bankrupt companies. Are you kidding? There's plenty of money – just look around. The intelligence agencies – all two dozen of them – should be dismantled and replaced with one effective group and really return intelligence to an organization. This will save huge amounts of the taxpayers' money. Apparently, those departments took a holiday on 9/11 – yet no one got terminated for dozing on the job.

What about cutting off pork? Read and weep about some of those outrageous overspending endeavors in the first chapter of *for seeing eye dogs only*. You can laugh about it, but the money came from your pockets and continues to do so. Too many of our taxpayer dollars – I send the government money from time to time – is wasted on the Department of Defense and corporate welfare. Corporations that rake in the profits don't need incentives or huge write-offs. Moreover, if they downsize and outsource jobs, they should be taxed, and fined as well. Those are the kinds of incentives the government should offer. The Department of

Homeland Obscurity investigation described earlier talks about more wasted spending. Why are taxes for the rich reduced when they ask not to have them lowered?

We have numerous problems: immigration, health care, social security, terrorism and security, intelligence, and employment in all its forms – including the minimum wage and the workweek. The citizens spoke in the U.S. elections of 2006 when they voted to immediately get the men and women in Iraq home. Why are they still there? This option will probably decrease terrorism there as well as in the United States and save billions of dollars. Another progressive idea to make terrorism a nuisance – yeah, Kerry was right – has to do with two courses of action.

The first is to get all those Americans stationed in foreign lands home. There is plenty of work for them here. The second idea is a new American service for the world, which creates high-paying jobs and helps other nations become self-sufficient. This is the new Peace Corps, without guns or uniforms. This is the alternative to sending bombs, weapons, foreign aid – which too often has turned into bullets – or even food, which may not get to where it is needed. Another suggestion is to reduce spending for defense. This country does not need to spend all that cash, especially with these two suggestions.

As I have already pointed out, there is money and plenty of it. Even more can be gotten by rescinding unfair taxes, increasing taxes where they should be levied, policing corrupt politicians and corporate criminals and that's only the beginning. Don't ignore my endless harping about cash sources. Not only can high-paying jobs be created, the goals of the thirty-hour workweek and the fifteen-dollar minimum wage can be reached, and we will solve a few problems besides. These challenges I have mentioned and in the process we can make the world a better place for everyone. However, we shouldn't stop there.

As you can see, we need a great deal of change and many individuals have to pitch in. Actually, many of them just have to do their job – these are the leeches in the companies who want a job without reporting for duty. However, we can all benefit from this effort. Corporations can rake in more money – even doing it without risking prison time for the CEOs – by lowering the workweek to thirty hours, paying people more and investing in green technologies and behaving *ethically*. I realize that's a new word for corporate America, but it can increase the bottom line. Cleaning up government results in a better workplace, shorter hours for everyone at the office, less pollution and healthier people with less stress. Lastly, getting rid of those obnoxious words, ***This Page Intentionally Left Blank*** means that the work force is more productive, they can retire sooner and we've destroyed fewer trees.

I close this book with a sighting. No, I didn't catch a glimpse of the King – he's in Tennessee doing Elvis impersonations. On Friday, November 17, 2006 I was on my way into the grocery store to pick up a few things – you may have guessed that it would end this way, but this is not about fruits, vegetables and meat. I spotted some windshield wipers on a car. You may feel that this isn't unusual except that they were on the headlights. On the way out of the store I noticed the car was a Volvo, but I didn't see any washer squirts. That will come with the next model.

References and recommended reading

Len Ackland – Making a Real Killing (1999: University of New Mexico Press)

Peter Harry Brown and Pat H. Broeske – The Untold Story of Howard Hughes (1996: Dutton – New York)

Bill Buford – Heat: an Amateur's Adventures as Kitchen Slave, Line Cook, Pasta Maker, and Apprentice to a Dante-quoting Butcher in Tuscany (2006: Knopf – New York)

Fred J. Cook – The Corrupted Land (1966: The Macmillan Company – New York)

Art Davidson – In the Wake of the Exxon Valdez (1990: Sierra Club Books – San Francisco)

Kenneth C. Davis – Don't Know Much about History (2003: HarperCollins – New York)

John de Graaf, editor – Take Back Your Time (2003: Berrett-Koehler Publishers – San Francisco)

Barbara Ehrenreich – Bait and Switch: the (Futile) Pursuit of the American Dream (2005: Henry Holt – New York)

Barbara Ehrenreich and Tamara Draut – *Downsized But Not Out*, The Nation magazine (November 6, 2006)

Barbara Ehrenreich – Nickel and Dimed: on not Getting by in America (2001: Henry Holt – New York)

Rafe Esquith – There are No Shortcuts (2003: Pantheon Books – New York)

Steven Freeman and Joel Bleifuss – Was the 2004 Presidential Election Stolen? Exit Polls, Election Fraud and the Official Count (2006: Seven Stories Press – New York)

Teri Garr with Henriette Mantel – Speedbumps: Flooring it through Hollywood (2005: Penguin – New York)

Lois Marie Gibbs – Love Canal: the Story Continues (1998: New Society Publishers – Gabriola Island, BC, Canada)

Richard N. Goodwin – Remembering America: a Voice from the Sixties (1988: Little, Brown – Boston)

Andrew M. Greeley – The Making of the Pope 2005: (2005: Little, Brown – New York)

Linda Greenlaw – All Fishermen are Liars: True Tales from the Dry Dock Bar (2004: Thorndike Press – Waterville, ME)

Linda Greenlaw – The Lobster Chronicles: Life on a Very Small Island (2002: Thorndike Press – Waterville, ME)

David I. Kertzer – The Popes against the Jews: the Vatican's Role in the Rise of Modern anti-Semitism (2001: Alfred A. Knopf – New York)

Peter Kurth – American Cassandra: The Life of Dorothy Thompson (1990: Little, Brown – Boston)

Dominique Lapierre and Javier Moro – Five past Midnight in Bhopal (2002: Warner Books – New York)

Paul Rogat Loeb – Soul of a Citizen: Living with Conviction in a Cynical Time (1999: St. Martins Griffin – New York)

Peter Manseau – Vows: the Story of a Priest, a Nun and Their Son (2005: Free Press – New York)

Joseph Marshall III – The Journey of Crazy Horse: a Lakota History (2004: Viking – New York)

Caroline Moorehead – Gelhorn: A Twentieth Century Life (2003: H. Holt – New York)

Lindsay Moran – Blowing my Cover: My Life as a CIA Spy (2005: Berkley Books – New York)

Ward Morehouse & M. Arun Subramaniam – The Bhopal Tragedy (1986: Council on International and Public Affairs – New York)

Richard F. Mould – Chernobyl: the Real Story (1988: Pergamon Press – New York)

Laurence J. Peter and Raymond Hull – The Peter principle (1969: Bantam Books – New York)

Ilene Philipson – Married to the Job: Why We Live to Work and What We Can Do about It (2002: The Free Press – New York)

Frank Rich – The Greatest Story Ever Sold: The Decline and Fall of Truth from 9/11 to Katrina (2006:The Penguin Group – New York)

Thomas E. Ricks – Fiasco: The American Military Adventure in Iraq (2006: The Penguin Press – New York)

Paul Robeson, Jr. – A Black Way of Seeing: from "Liberty" to Freedom (2006: Seven Stories Press – New York)

Karenna Gore Schiff – Lighting the Way: 9 Women Who Changed Modern America (2005: Miramax Books / Hyperion – New York)

Eric Schlosser – Fast Food Nation: the Dark Side of the All-American Meal (2001: Houghton Mifflin – Boston)

Upton Sinclair – The Jungle (1988: Peachtree – Memphis)

David Sirota – Hostile Takeover: How Big Money & Corruption Conquered Our Government – and How We Take It Back (2006: Crown Publishers – New York)

Douglas B. Sosnik, Matthew J. Dowd & Ron Fournier – Applebee's America: How Successful Political, Business, and Religious Leaders Connect with the New American Community (2006: Simon & Schuster – New York)

Helene Stapinski – Five-finger Discount: A Crooked Family History (2001: Random House – New York)

Willie Sutton – Where the Money Was (1976: Viking Press – York)

Robert S. Swiatek – Don't Bet On It (2003: Infinity Publishing – Haverford, PA)

Robert S. Swiatek – for seeing eye dogs only (2005: Aventine Press – San Diego)

Robert S. Swiatek – The Read My Lips Cookbook: a Culinary Journey of Memorable Meals (2002: Infinity Publishing – Haverford, PA)

Robert S. Swiatek – Tick Tock, Don't Stop: a Manual for
Workaholics (2003: Infinity Publishing – Haverford, PA)

Helen Thomas – Front Row at the White House: My Life and
Times (1999: A Lisa Drew Book – New York)

Helen Thomas – Watchdogs of Democracy: the Waning
Washington Press Corps and How it Has Failed the Public
(2006: Scribner – New York)

Morris West – The Clowns of God (1981: Morrow – New
York)

Bob Woodward – State of Denial: Bush at War, Part III (2006:
Simon & Schuster – New York)

Mike Wright – What They Didn't Teach You about the (2001:
Presidio – Novato, CA)

David A. Yallop – In God's Name: an Investigation into the
Murder of John Paul I (1984: Bantam Books – Toronto)

Alla Yaroshinskaya – Chernobyl: the Forbidden Truth (1995:
University of Nebraska Press – Lincoln)

Printed in the United States
200094BV00002B/436-594/A